The Paris Manuscript

OTHER TITLES IN THE THEATRE
MAKERS SERIES INCLUDE:

The Theatre and its Double by Antonin Artaud and translated by Mark Taylor-Batty

Theatre across Borders by Abhishek Majumdar

Notes from the Rehearsal Room: A Director's Process by Nancy Meckler

Toward a Future Theatre: Conversations during a Pandemic by Caridad Svich

The Uncapturable: The Fleeting Art of Theatre by Rubén Szuchmacher and translated by William Gregory

Adrian Lester and Lolita Chakrabarti: A Working Diary by Adrian Lester and Lolita Chakrabarti

Movement Directors in Contemporary Theatre: Conversations on Craft by Ayse Tashkiran

Contemporary Women Stage Directors: Conversations on Craft by Paulette Marty

Julie Hesmondhalgh: A Working Diary by Julie Hesmondhalgh

Julius Caesar and Me: Exploring Shakespeare's African Play by Peterson Joseph

The Actor and His Body by Litz Pisk and introduction by Ayse Tashkiran

Steppenwolf Theatre Company of Chicago: In Their Own Words by John Mayer

The Paris Manuscript

The Early Draft Rediscovered

Michael Chekhov

Translated with an introduction and 'Reflections From the Studio' by Hugo Moss

methuen | drama
LONDON · NEW YORK · OXFORD · NEW DELHI · SYDNEY

METHUEN DRAMA
Bloomsbury Publishing Plc
50 Bedford Square, London, WC1B 3DP, UK
1385 Broadway, New York, NY 10018, USA
29 Earlsfort Terrace, Dublin 2, Ireland

BLOOMSBURY, METHUEN DRAMA and the Methuen Drama logo are trademarks of Bloomsbury Publishing Plc

First published in Great Britain 2025

Copyright © The Estate of Michael Chekhov and Hugo Moss, 2025

The Estate of Michael Chekhov and Hugo Moss have asserted their right under the Copyright, Designs and Patents Act, 1988, to be identified as authors of this work.

For legal purposes the Acknowledgements on pp. xxi–xxii constitute an extension of this copyright page.

Cover design: Ben Anslow
Cover image source: Boner Georgette Nachlass

All rights reserved. No part of this publication may be reproduced or transmitted in any form or by any means, electronic or mechanical, including photocopying, recording, or any information storage or retrieval system, without prior permission in writing from the publishers.

Bloomsbury Publishing Plc does not have any control over, or responsibility for, any third-party websites referred to or in this book. All internet addresses given in this book were correct at the time of going to press. The author and publisher regret any inconvenience caused if addresses have changed or sites have ceased to exist, but can accept no responsibility for any such changes.

Every effort has been made to trace copyright holders and to obtain their permission for the use of copyright material. However, if any have been inadvertently overlooked, the publishers will be pleased, if notified of any omissions, to make the necessary arrangement at the first opportunity.

A catalogue record for this book is available from the British Library.

A catalog record for this book is available from the Library of Congress

ISBN: HB: 978-1-3504-3738-8
PB: 978-1-3504-3737-1
ePDF: 978-1-3504-3739-5
eBook: 978-1-3504-3740-1

Series: Theatre Makers

Typeset by Integra Software Services Pvt. Ltd.
Printed and bound in Great Britain

To find out more about our authors and books visit www.bloomsbury.com and sign up for our newsletters.

hdk
Zürcher Hochschule der Künste
Zurich University of the Arts

This book has been made possible thanks to a collaboration between Michael Chekhov Brasil and the Institute for the Performing Arts and Film (IPF), Zurich University of the Arts.

subTexte Band 32 der Zürcher Hochschule der Künste.
info.ipf@zhdk.ch | https://blog.zhdk.ch/subtexte/

Permission to publish extracts from the archive 'Actor is the Theatre: a collection of Michael Chekhov's unpublished notes and manuscripts on the art of acting and the theatre: typescript 1977' is granted by courtesy of the Estate of Deirdre Hurst du Prey.

The poem *The Metamorphosis of Artists* by Thaís Loureiro was first published in a 2020 eBook by the Michael Chekhov School in partnership with Michael Chekhov Brasil.

Epigraph by E.M. Cioran © 2024 Skyhorse Publishing Inc.

for Thaís
(tautology)

CONTENTS

List of Illustrations xiii
Preface xvi
Acknowledgements xxi

Introduction 1
Editing and Abridging Chekhov's Text 15
Translating Chekhov's German 17
   Seelisch, geistig 19
   Gestalt 21
   Weltanschauung and *Weltempfindung* 21

A Memo to the Reader 25

The 'Paris Manuscript' 27
   Attention 28
   Movement 32
   Imagination 37
   Speech 41
   Seelisch Atmosphere 45
   Rhythm 48
   Artistic Individuality 52
   Weltanschauung 56
   Theatre Now and in the Future 60
   Character and Destiny 69
   Gestalt 73

A Path – First Stage 77
A Path – Second Stage 89
A Path – Third Stage 100
A Path – Fourth Stage 105
Afterword 108

Reflections from the Studio 111
    La petite bergère 112
    The First Condition 116
    A Gift Received 120
    More Concrete than a Memory, More Organized than a Dream 125
    Goethe's Method for Observing Natural Phenomena 127
    Seelische Geste 130
    A Play Going on in My Head 135
    Course Made Good 140
    Thinking Feeling Willing 144
    A Meditation 149
    From *The Metamorphosis of Artists* 152

Appendix 156
    Georgette Boner 156
    Michael Chekhov Brasil 158
    The Four Manuscripts 159
    Further Study 162
Notes 166
Bibliography 178
Index 181

ILLUSTRATIONS

Except where otherwise stated, all illustrations are from the Boner Georgette Nachlass archives, Institute for the Performing Arts and Film (IPF), Zurich University of the Arts (ZHdK), Switzerland.

Front cover Michael Chekhov. Paris, probably 1931

Frontispiece Michael Chekhov. Riga, 1932

1 Michael Chekhov. Baldone, 1932 2
2 Michael Chekhov and Georgette Boner. Baldone, 1932 2
3 Michael Chekhov. Baldone, 1932 2
4 Xenia and Michael Chekhov. Latvia, 1934 2
5 Xenia and Michael Chekhov. Birzgale, 1934 2
6 Michael Chekhov. Baldone, 1932 3
7 Georgette Boner and Michael Chekhov. Latvia, 1932 4
8 Xenia and Michael Chekhov. Venice, 1934 6
9 Michael and Xenia Chekhov, Alice and Georgette Boner. Venice, 1934 6
10 Georgette Boner with her father and Michael Chekhov. Venice, 1934 6
11 Michael and Xenia Chekhov. Venice, 1934 6
12 Michael Chekhov. Venice, 1934 6
13 Michael and Xenia Chekhov. Venice, 1934 6
14 Page 209 of the 'Paris Manuscript' 16
15 Venn diagram: *seelisch* vs. *geistig* elements of the human experience. Illustration by Beatrice Moss. Michael Chekhov Brasil archive 20
16 The first surviving page of the 'Paris Manuscript' 27
17 Page 30 of the 'Paris Manuscript' 34
18 Page 40 of the 'Paris Manuscript' 42
19 Page 70 of the 'Paris Manuscript' 49

20 Page 119 of the 'Paris Manuscript' 54
21 Page 143 of the 'Paris Manuscript' 61
22 Original diagram on page 163 of the 'Paris Manuscript' 68
23 Page 181 of the 'Paris Manuscript' 76
24 Original diagram on page 207 of the 'Paris Manuscript' 84
25 Page 228 of the 'Paris Manuscript' 91
26 Page 292 of the 'Paris Manuscript' 97
27 Page 329 of the 'Paris Manuscript' 103
28 Last page of the 'Paris Manuscript' (numbered 350 & 351) 110
29 Jean-Jacques Henner. *La petite bergère*, c. 1890. Photo © Musée d'Unterlinden, Dist. RMN-Grand Palais/image Musée Unterlinden de Colmar 113
30 'Goblet' diagram from du Prey's transcription of Chekhov's 19 May 1936 class, Estate of Deirdre Hurst du Prey 120
31 Sketch I in the 'Paris Manuscript' 121
32 Sketch II in the 'Paris Manuscript' 121
33 Sketch III in the 'Paris Manuscript' 122
34 Sketch V in the 'Paris Manuscript' 122
35 Sketch VI in the 'Paris Manuscript' 123
36 *Theatre Arts Monthly*, January 1937 (inside cover). Michael Chekhov Brasil archive 132
37 Course steered vs. course made good. Illustration by Beatrice Moss. Michael Chekhov Brasil archive 142
38 Threefold nature of inspiration. Figure illustration: Estate Georgette Boner archives 146
39 Threefold negative and positive forces. Figure illustration: Estate Georgette Boner archives 148
40 Focused and open attention in meditation. Illustration by editor/author. Michael Chekhov Brasil archive 149

What will be the physiognomy of painting, of poetry, of music in a hundred years? No one can tell. As after the fall of Athens, of Rome, a long pause will intervene, caused by the exhaustion of the means of expression, as well as by the exhaustion of consciousness itself. Humanity, to rejoin the past, must invent a second naiveté, without which the arts can never begin again.[1]

E. M. CIORAN

PREFACE

From the early 2010s and for nearly a decade my partner Thaís Loureiro and I explored Michael Chekhov's artistic legacy as teachers, directors and performers, at the studio that we founded together in Rio de Janeiro, Michael Chekhov Brasil. We also took this work around the country, often through partnerships with institutions such as Unicamp (State University of Campinas), SESC and other collaborations, and while teaching thousands of actors the fundamentals of Chekhov's approach to their craft and to a great extent putting his work on the map of theatre practice in Brazil for the first time, we constantly engaged with the question of how much of the philosophy underpinning the 'technique', the body of the iceberg, so to speak, lying under the surface and supporting the various exercises, we should/could include in our programmes.

As well as having been blessed to find several wonderful teachers of our own, Thaís and I were greatly inspired early on by the discovery of the vast archive of Chekhov's lessons and lectures that Deirdre Hurst du Prey transcribed almost from her very first meeting with him in 1935, and right up to the early 1940s.[2] On the evidence of these records, Chekhov's own teaching put a great deal of emphasis on encouraging the development of independent artists through a particular awareness and refined connection to the world of their own imagination and creative self, and less on teaching a canon of exercises to be called upon as a handy way of, say, creating character or colouring a scenic moment. In his hands, the exercises appear to be aimed at precisely strengthening this broader formation of the group as individual artists and as an ensemble, into and through which elements such as character, gesture, atmosphere and so forth might flow and find free expression.

We also took very much to heart the keynote address that Andrei Kirillov gave during a 2005 symposium at Dartington Hall (published the following year under the title 'Michael Chekhov and the Search for the "Ideal" Theatre'). It is worth quoting Kirillov at length:

> While preparing for this symposium, [the organizers] suggested we answer the provocative question: 'Does Chekhov's system still have any impact on the real needs of modern theatre practice, or is it the outdated fantasy of that gentleman alone?' Grasping this provocation, I throw back my own counter-provocation. Are we ready to answer this question? And from which point, from what dimension, are we ready to answer it? What do we mean when we talk about Chekhov's theatre system? Do we mean a collection of his exercises, which are really very helpful? ... But the physical execution of these exercises to the very letter of Chekhov's description often has nothing in common with Chekhov's 'theatre ideology'. For example, the famous exercise with the balls: we can throw the balls to each other for ages and even form a good volleyball team, but this will change nothing in our artistic skills.[3]

Thaís and I took these questions seriously and recognized the importance of engaging with and responding to what is certainly a stark caution. But Kirillov goes further:

> I maintain that it is possible to execute any exercise and any action on the theatre stage in accordance with Chekhov's theatre ideology. At the same time, every one of his exercises can be executed without any connection to this ideology, or with a wrong understanding of both the ideology and the connection ... There is a real danger of splitting Chekhov's theatre system into a number of discrete devices and tools ... However, if this tendency triumphs over the wholeness of the system, Chekhov's theatre ideology will die instantly. Life is hectic and, as professionals, we are in a permanent rush ... Alas, as long as we are in a rush Chekhov cannot help us. As long as we are 'practical' only, the pure idealist Chekhov will not answer our questions. We will use not more then five per cent of the advantages of his theatre and his theatre system. Chekhov's theatre likes dreamers, idealists who desire and have time for *meditation*, which is the

real ideology of his magic theatre. Stripped of this ideology, his exercises will simply be exercises, and these tools will not show their mystery in depth.[4]

It is probably worth pointing out that Mala Powers, who knew Chekhov well in the last years of his life and, following his death, was the executrix of his estate, helped review the text of Kirillov's talk and, I think we might therefore surmise, will have shared some of these concerns.

I wouldn't presume to attempt a comprehensive review of today's landscape of Michael Chekhov's legacy from Kirillov's standpoint, beyond generalizing – I hope not controversially – that while the study of a canon of exercises widely recognized as the Chekhov Technique is now accessible in many parts of the world and growing in popularity, something we can certainly celebrate, penetrating the broader horizon and depths of what Kirillov terms his 'ideology' is far less widespread. Of course, certain exercises fit more readily into the existing frameworks and time constraints of teaching programmes and rehearsal practice, while the philosophy behind them, our engagement with the human creative process and development as artists, takes far more time and indeed always requires a distinct, individual, holistic approach. Naturally, such matters go well beyond the confines of this or that technique label and, as Chekhov emphasized throughout his life, must be discovered by all artists, regardless of their field and background.

Clearly an individual exercise can be led in such a way that it does awaken the fundamental elements of Chekhov's 'ideology', the creative individuality, artistic self, and personal growth, but we would still be wise to heed Kirillov's overall point that existing teaching structures, academic programmes and time constraints naturally present obstacles, and may even facilitate a Chinese whispers type spread of exercises 'without any connection to [the] ideology, or with a wrong understanding of both the ideology and the connection'.[5] Nowadays research online of the Michael Chekhov Technique will turn up any a number of 'fool-proof' tutorials based on the exercises for quickly accessing states or making acting choices, but as Aldous Huxley has wisely pointed out, all that is fool-proof is invariably also grace-proof,[6] and something we should surely never lose sight of is that, as artists, our work must ultimately strive for that which cannot be expressed merely through craft.

The Sufi teacher and author Idries Shah, writing in a quite different context, makes an insightful point regarding the dynamic of bringing practices and methods of a certain characteristic into frameworks of a divers or even contrasting nature:

> If you adopt the methods or institutions which have been developed by people with one set of ideas, these methods or institutions will eventually take over. The result will be that your ideas or objectives will be overcome by the ideas which were originally present in the instrument which you tried to adapt. This principle may be seen throughout human history. A religion, for instance, which adopts the structures and procedures of another will end up resembling the previous one far more than itself. If it has prevailed over another religion in the same area, it will develop the same old-age symptoms or weaknesses as the original one. All that the second religion will have contributed is a certain amount of energy, which will soon be spent.[7]

The 'Paris Manuscript' is certainly a significant historical document for anyone interested in Michael Chekhov's life and work, but perhaps its publication may also provide an opportunity for many actors, artists and teachers to take a moment to (re)connect with, deepen their knowledge of and respond personally to this side of Chekhov's legacy, the submerged part of the 'iceberg', the artist's creative and spiritual self, whose concentration, imagination, artistic outlook and so forth require constant nourishment. Ideally these will support our practice more consciously and tangibly than the existing structures and 'permanent rush' of modern life often allow. In the last section of the book, Reflections From the Studio, I share a few of the discoveries and practices that Thaís and I explored as they relate to one or two central themes found in Chekhov's ur-text, which despite its unfinished state contains plenty of material for independent-minded newcomers and aficionados alike, if only we are able to slow down enough and through such explorations find not all the answers (one would hope), but get the most out of our seeking.

It is worth stating that like Chekhov's original text, this book has been created first and foremost out of a personal desire to engage with actors and artists. Indeed, the initial impulse to translate a few sections of the 'Paris Manuscript' was to share and explore them with actors in workshops, so this volume is presented in the same spirit, as a direct sourcebook for theatre people and others, a natural extension of over a decade of creative work at our studio. Having said that, the Introduction does present a fair amount of historical context, with a narrative of the relevant period of Chekhov's life, an account of why I myself find the 'Paris Manuscript' of particular relevance today and my overall approach to editing the text. So if this background material is of secondary interest to any actors reading this, I won't mind in the slightest if you skip discreetly ahead to Chekhov's text (and from there on to our own Reflections From the Studio) – you will, though, first have to take a quick look at a couple of important points relating to the translation (see under 'Translating Chekhov's German').

ACKNOWLEDGEMENTS

My thanks must begin with Fern Sloan and Joanna Merlin, who over a few icy days in early January 2010 drew a line in both the Galway snow and my life, a threshold across which I ended up discovering a vast and beautiful world of artistic exploration, and also of love.

I am grateful for the creative inspiration and practical support that my partner Thaís Loureiro and I continued to receive from Joanna and Fern during the early years of the Michael Chekhov Brasil initiative and beyond, as well as from the MICHA Michael Chekhov Association family as a whole and in various ways, among them Dawn Arnold, Marjolein Baars, Bethany Caputo, Jessica Cerullo, Ragnar Freidank, John McManus, Lenard Petit, Ted Pugh and David Zinder. Just as the revision work of the typescript was being completed, news of Joanna Merlin's passing at the age of ninety-two reached us, and now on the eve of the typeset book being sent to print, we learn that Lenard Petit has also sadly left us. I take this opportunity to pay special tribute to these two friends and teachers who gave so generously to the Michael Chekhov community the world over.

Over the years our work in Brazil has been made all the richer by the mentorship of Jobst Langhans (Michael Tschechow Studio Berlin, Germany); the deep-felt personal connection to the Michael Chekhov School (Hudson, New York); our association with the Michael Chekhov Acting School (New York); and our friendship with Sarah Kane (Performing Arts International, UK).

I want to thank every artist who attended the workshops that Thaís and I gave around Brazil throughout the 2010s, and without whom none of our work would have been possible; Veronica Fabrini of Unicamp (State University of Campinas) for the years of collaboration and friendship; the four groups of the Bases online workshops that from 2020 worked with such dedication through the Covid-19 pandemic and beyond (a special thanks also to our international guests Joanna Merlin, Fern Sloan and Ted Pugh, Marjolein Baars, Sarah Kane, and John McManus); and I particularly wish to record my deepest thanks to and admiration for my colleagues and very dear friends Amparo de Gata, Bruna Mafra, Dani Kupek, Fran Mattoso and Rô Milani. It is largely thanks to their love and dedication that Michael Chekhov Brasil has continued to radiate so strong and far since Thaís's sudden passing in September 2019.

I am grateful to Prof. Anton Rey (Institute for the Performing Arts and Film, ZHdK), both for his initial encouragement and the very generous support provided throughout the development of the 'Paris Manuscript' project, and thanks to Rolf Wolfensberger and all the staff at Archiv ZHdK for making the Estate Georgette Boner archives freely available over numerous visits. For assisting research my thanks also go out to the librarians at: Billy Rose Theatre Division, New York Public Library (Deirdre Hurst du Prey's 'The Actor is the Theatre' archive and the Beatrice Straight Papers); Devon Heritage Centre, Exeter ('Michael Chekhov Studio Deirdre Hurst du Prey Archive'); and Kent State University Library (Robert Lewis Papers).

For a wide range of invaluable practical, professional and moral support my warm-hearted thanks radiate out to Beatrice, Bella, Margi, Gérard, Mary and Guy Moss (the last three *in memoriam*), Janine Desmeusles and Brigitte Bettex, Jacky Inglis, Linda Worrell-Wraight and Peter Wraight, Bernadette Wintsch-Heinen and Mani Wintsch, Paula Alegria, Daniela Sirkin, Hadar Be'hochma, Cleiton Echeveste, Sol Garre, Pedro Telles, Anouk Magara, Ion Mills and Hannah Patterson, Niranjan Rajah and Nadine Freysz.

For permission to publish extracts from Deirdre Hurst du Prey's archive my renewed thanks go to Pierre du Prey; thanks to Musée Unterlinden in Colmar and RMN Grand Palais for permission to reproduce *La petite bergère* by Jean-Jacques Henner; and lastly (this only because these acknowledgements have turned out to be broadly speaking chronological) I extend my gracious thanks to Kim Barrett Lane, executrix of the Michael Chekhov Estate, for her immediate friendship and generous support in getting another of Chekhov's texts into print; and to my editor Anna Brewer and the rest of the team at Bloomsbury (among them Aanchal Vij, production editor Elizabeth Kellingley, project manager Rebecca Willford, copyeditor Dawn Cunneen, proofreader Peter Stafford and designer Ben Anslow) for all their hard work and patient guidance throughout the book's publishing journey.

Introduction

The 'Paris Manuscript' is a document in the Estate Georgette Boner archives held in the vaults of the Zurich University of the Arts (ZHdK) in Switzerland. It is the photocopy of a manuscript that Michael Chekhov wrote by hand in German in (as far as one can tell) medium-sized notebooks,[8] with amendments and revision marks throughout, many paragraphs rewritten and glued over each other, as well as several pages taped together to form long folded sheets. Pagination marks are visible on most pages and the frequently revised sequence runs up to 351. It is not clear when the photocopy was made but it was among the papers entrusted to ZHdK in late 2008 by Dr Ambros Boner, a cousin of the Swiss theatre director and artist Georgette Boner. By January 2009, the collection had already been organized and catalogued to the highest standards by Peter K. Jakob, and in addition to this manuscript the archive contains a considerable assortment of personal photographs, letters and papers, both relating to Chekhov and other material from Boner's long life.

Boner and Chekhov met in Paris on 17 May 1931 and they became lifelong friends, collaborating on several projects in the 1930s, among them this literary work, which was Chekhov's first far-reaching attempt at writing about the actor's craft. The archived copy of the 'Paris Manuscript' carries a cover sheet indicating that it was written between 1932 and 1934; however, as we shall see, the title itself may be somewhat misleading, because from early 1932 Chekhov lived and worked in the Baltic states of Latvia and Lithuania, and according to Boner their collaboration on the text only began that summer when she visited Chekhov and

FIGURE 1 *Michael Chekhov. Baldone, 1932.*
FIGURE 2 *Michael Chekhov and Georgette Boner. Baldone, 1932.*
FIGURE 3 *Michael Chekhov. Baldone, 1932.*

FIGURE 4 *Xenia and Michael Chekhov. Latvia, 1934.*
FIGURE 5 *Xenia and Michael Chekhov. Birzgale, 1934.*

his wife Xenia in Riga. Bar tours in 1933 to Estonia and Poland, the Chekhovs appear to have remained in Kaunas and Riga until September 1934, and the numerous side comments and notes to Boner scribbled throughout the manuscript indicate that Chekhov would write sections and forward them to her for comment and eventual revision.[9]

In January 1934, Chekhov suffered a heart attack. In *Life and Encounters*, the memoirs he completed a decade later, he describes the subsequent months of convalescence as being a time of reflection and discovery, and from this account we are able follow some invaluable insights developing, among them observations about the natural world that would certainly go on to feed into the series of explorations that actors the world over now know as Psychological Gesture:

> Lying in the garden on bright, sunny days, I observed the harmonious forms of the planets, I imagined the process of the rotation of the Earth around the planets, I searched for harmonious compositions in space and gradually came to the experience of *movement, invisible to the external eye* that is present in all phenomena in the world. There even seemed to me to be such movement in motionless, solidified forms. It was movement that had created form and still maintained it ... it was as if I were witnessing some creative process: whatever I looked at seemed to be in the process of coming into being before my very eyes. I called this invisible movement, this play of forces, 'gesture'.[10]

However, in the manuscript the frequent self-deprecating side notes to Boner (one section ends with the aside: 'Stupidly expressed. Help please! How can you possibly bear all this!') attest to the fact that Chekhov was struggling to put into words the complex ideas about the human creative process – and not for the first time, having previously been forced to admit in a letter of apology to a group of young Lithuanian actors that a promised text on rhythm had produced nothing but a messy tangle of ideas.[11] The memoirs go on:

FIGURE 6 *Michael Chekhov. Baldone, 1932.*

> The philosophical system that had started to take shape in my mind ... was so complex that the idea of applying it to theatre art was out of the question. I myself, possibly, could use it for ... acting on stage, but how was I going to explain it

to other people? ... Actors, and in particular good actors, shy away from all the discussions, systems and methods that theatre theoreticians are keen to impose on them ... and I myself had created a system that was probably unintelligible without a knowledge of natural science and astronomy! I felt miserable. But then I found unexpected relief – in the form of a listener.[12]

This was Boner, who in July 1934 returned to join Chekhov and Xenia in Riga, and it is my understanding that it was over the next several weeks that the bulk of the revision and organization of the 'Paris Manuscript' as we now have it must have taken place. Chekhov's remark that the relief was 'unexpected' may be a minor simplification for narrative purposes, or an indication that up to that point he had simply been sending off the accumulation of unsatisfactory texts to Boner, without as yet much useful exchange back and forth, nor indeed hope of finding any real light at the end of the tunnel. Be that as it may, Chekhov clearly still had grave misgivings about the value of the texts being produced, and he recalls that it was entirely thanks to Boner's arrival that summer that he did finally begin to find a path for formulating the chaos of ideas in his mind, writing that 'she was gifted, witty and had a rich and lively imagination', and could elevate him to great 'philosophical heights with her questions, advice and arguments'.[13]

FIGURE 7 *Georgette Boner and Michael Chekhov. Latvia, 1932.*

I think it would be hard to exaggerate Boner's contribution, if not to Chekhov's artistic development as such, then certainly to his ability to get his mind around the form of his burgeoning artistic vision and begin to express it clearly, both theoretically and in the more practical terms that others might be able to follow. The thirty-nine-year-old man pictured on the cover of this book, who arrived in the Baltic from Paris a few months after that photo was taken, was already one of the greatest living actors, but the Michael Chekhov that emerged two years later was fundamentally transformed. Although physically debilitated by his recent health scare, the breadth and clarity of his artistic and philosophical vision had now grown beyond all recognition, and with Boner's help and encouragement he had finally managed to set down in writing a comprehensive draft of these ideas. Indeed, I strongly suspect Boner's skill in encouraging Chekhov to focus and organize his ideas about the creative process, in addition to all that he had experienced teaching, performing and directing in Riga and Kaunas, would ultimately be decisive in giving Chekhov the confidence, several months later, to accept the invitation to join the progressive 'Dartington Experiment' at Dartington Hall, in Devon, England,[14] with the creation of the Chekhov Theatre Studio.

The last time that Chekhov and Boner might have had the opportunity to do any real work on the book would have been when she and her sister, the artist Alice Boner, accompanied Chekhov and Xenia to Italy, from September 1934. Rather like in 1928, when the couple had had to flee the Soviet Union, the Chekhovs were suddenly forced out of Latvia for political reasons, this time following a coup d'état that established an authoritarian, nationalist dictatorship and left their position in the country untenable. They travelled via Berlin to southern Germany to visit their good friend Margareta Morgenstern,[15] before continuing south to Venice so that Chekhov could continue his convalescence in a warmer climate. There the group was joined by the Boner sisters' father, and in late October they visited the spa town of Salsomaggiore Terme, near Parma, to take the waters. Then in early December the Chekhovs and Georgette Boner returned to Paris, with Chekhov evidently just about well enough to throw himself into preparations for the US tour that was suddenly being arranged for the spring, including trial performances in Brussels just after the New Year.[16] In mid-February 1935, a few days after their ship sailed into New York harbour, Chekhov, Xenia and Boner met two young women who would turn out to play their own key roles in his life and later legacy, Beatrice Straight and Deirdre Hurst. Indeed it was thanks to them that the tour turned out to be fruitful in more ways than anyone could have imagined: by the late spring the Chekhovs were already starting to prepare for the move to England and the Dartington Hall adventure that would begin the following year, and so at the end of May Boner returned to Paris alone (although she would later visit the Chekhovs at Dartington, on several occasions gave lectures there,

FIGURE 8 *Xenia and Michael Chekhov. Venice, 1934.*

FIGURE 9 *Michael and Xenia Chekhov, Alice and Georgette Boner. Venice, 1934.*

FIGURE 10 *Georgette Boner with her father and Michael Chekhov. Venice, 1934.*

FIGURE 11 *Michael and Xenia Chekhov. Venice, 1934.*

FIGURE 12 *Michael Chekhov. Venice, 1934.*

FIGURE 13 *Michael and Xenia Chekhov. Venice, 1934.*

and would remain close to this family of artist friends right through to the end of her life).

It therefore seems highly likely that not a single line of what has long been known as the 'Paris Manuscript' was actually written in the French capital (unless perhaps Chekhov and Boner managed to work on the text during those few busy weeks leading up to the US tour). What is not in doubt is that it was in Paris that the manuscript was left behind in its unfinished state, to all intents and purposes abandoned and apparently forgotten by all but its guardian, Boner (and it was surely she that at some point gave the document its name, perhaps more as a note to self than a descriptive title as such). Chekhov meanwhile had by the summer begun working on an identical writing project, this time in English with Hurst acting as scribe, and although it appears she wasn't even aware of a previous German text until several decades later,[17] neither can we ignore the abundant evidence of how little there is in Chekhov's subsequent writings and teaching work that did not build on what he and Boner had begun to explore in the 'Paris Manuscript',[18] which despite its incomplete and unpolished state nevertheless presents us with a fully formed ontology of the human creative process as it relates to actors, a firm foundation for all that was to come.

Here are ur-texts on concentration, imagination, atmosphere, radiating, gesture, a quartet that Chekhov later baptized the 'Four Brothers' (feeling of ease, form, beauty and sense of the whole), qualities of movement, discussions of thinking, feeling, willing, of 'what' versus 'how', the problems of naturalism in art and bringing personal everyday experiences or memories into our work as raw material, and we also come across early versions of the four stages of the creative process, leading questions, archetypes (the term is never actually used, but the premise does appear here in more than one guise) and a host of other elements that form a constant seam running across Chekhov's entire teaching work at Dartington and Ridgefield (Connecticut, where the Studio moved in 1939), the three books about acting that he did complete, and right through to the lectures he recorded in Hollywood shortly before his life was prematurely cut short by another heart attack, in September 1955, a month after his sixty-fourth birthday.[19]

In addition to all this familiar material, Chekhov gives an evocative depiction here of precisely what it is an actor encounters in a moment of inspiration (clearly writing from deep personal experience), and discusses topics as varied as speech formation; the so-called lawfulness of our creative consciousness; the relationship between dreams and artistic creation; what he terms the 'technical-professional' importance of attending to the artist's endlessly developing overall perception of the world around (*Weltanschauung*); and how as we first approach a play it is not a void that we encounter, but rather a vastness containing 'the whole world, the entire past, present and future characters with their destinies ... It contains all. And therefore it is completely empty' [83]. The 'Paris Manuscript' also contains beautiful insights that I for one had not come across in later writings, for instance the somewhat aphoristic observation that in everyday life a liar who 'gives a good performance' is always concealing something, whereas on stage a good performance is the polar opposite, a complete revelation; so an artistic lie on stage (a bad performance) means the actors are concealing something and consequently the audience are unable to take them seriously as characters [46]. There are many other gems like this along the way.

However, it cannot be denied that the document lying among Georgette Boner's theatre papers in Switzerland does present a few problematic issues, the first being the mystery of the whereabouts of Chekhov's original handwritten notebooks (as has already been mentioned, the version we have is only a photocopy). During the 1970s George Shdanoff,[20] his long-time collaborator, lobbied to have any papers collected and archived in Moscow, so one theory that has been mooted is that the original was among material that he persuaded Boner to send there.[21] Similarly, Deirdre Hurst du Prey (as she became following her marriage) was at that time organizing her own papers and making efforts to collect in Dartington as many of the surviving papers from Chekhov's exile years as possible;[22] however, there is no record of his handwritten manuscript at the Devon Heritage Centre in Exeter, where this archive is now kept. It has occurred to me that the very existence of a photocopy of the 'Paris Manuscript' may itself be an indication that Boner parted with the original, or intended to, but none of these considerations rises above mere conjecture, and bar some new development the whereabouts of this relic will remain an enigma.

Furthermore, the photocopy that we do have appears to be incomplete, since the text makes reference to an introductory chapter (or foreword) and an annex of practical exercises. We cannot be certain that either of these texts was actually written,[23] but if so, both are missing from the Zurich archive, as are a group of four consecutive pages from the middle of the manuscript[24] and a series of five drawings.[25] Another issue is that, as has also already been noted, work was never completed and the text is clearly still an unpolished early draft, uneven in quality, with some repetition and occasional lack of clarity, not least because Chekhov's handwriting and the numerous amendments aren't always that easy to decipher. Considering all this, one could surely be forgiven for presuming the 'Paris Manuscript' to be of limited interest: a rough, never finished, incomplete – and merely second-hand – record of one of Chekhov's abandoned projects during the early years of his long exile from the Soviet Union. For many researchers and historians this may very well be the case, and indeed more than one previous commentator has lamented particularly the loss of the annex of exercises.[26] However, as an artist, teacher and seeker who has been inspired by Michael Chekhov for many years now, two aspects of this unique document have come to overshadow, at least for me, its undeniable flaws. As it happens, at first glance both might also be seen as representing disadvantages, but placed at a certain angle to the light they turn out to have much to reveal.

The first is the language, German, which as is widely known allows one to vary the word order a great deal, depending on the desired emphasis, while providing an often surprising range of synonyms to reflect the subtlest of shades of a great many concepts, in addition to the seemingly endless possibilities for stringing together compound words – even allowing the odd brand new one to be plucked out of nowhere with little danger of ambiguity. However, Chekhov's mother tongue was, of course, Russian and writing in a foreign language, as many of us know from personal experience, can be a considerable challenge. But, whereas in nearly all of his later work he had to contend with English, here he was able to make the most of a language particularly well suited to expressing abstract or complex philosophical ideas with considerable precision. Despite being prone to getting a little muddled and verbose in his navigation of written German (and his spelling certainly leaves something to be desired), Chekhov's wide vocabulary and fluent command of the language are nevertheless unmistakable, and as I've studied this text my overall impression has been that Chekhov was at greater ease expressing himself in German than ever was the case with English.

As well as presenting a vision of the actor's creative process, the 'Paris Manuscript' contains some profound insights into the way materialism had already begun to affect an artist's path to inspiration, with Chekhov sharing prescient concerns about the ways in which the growing mechanization of society would come to further shift this dynamic for actors, and I believe that his mastery of German as a vehicle for thinking things through, together with having found in Georgette Boner such a gifted and curious artistic interlocutor, constitute a bequest well worthy of our attention still today. Furthermore, the text reveals Chekhov getting the most out of some of the resources of the German language, in particular through his use of the words *seelisch* and *geistig* to refer to what he viewed (and experienced) as two distinct aspects or regions of our non-physical, spiritual life. English has no precise equivalent for these, and since working with and developing our incorporeal, inner life actually forms the bedrock of Chekhov's approach to the actor's craft generally, this turns out to be of considerable significance for our practical work. We shall return presently to take a look at the meaning of these and a couple of other German expressions that Chekhov uses to great effect, and which have in turn shaped the English translation.

The second reason I find the 'Paris Manuscript' valuable, despite its flaws, is that it was clearly Chekhov's first concerted attempt at getting such a wide scope of ideas about the workings of the actor's craft down onto paper. His first and worst attempt, some might respond (including quite possibly, it must be said, Chekhov himself). Nevertheless, the more I have studied this early draft text and having, through the long process of editing and abridging, moved beyond the handwritten scrawl, faltering spelling, the uneven first draft presentation of themes and some otherwise less accomplished pages generally, the stronger my impression that its unpolished state also represents a rare gift: a privileged fly-on-the-wall glimpse of the dawning of an artistic genius's creative vision. Although the form of how to present everything was clearly still a work in progress, what Chekhov puts into this text is also correspondingly fresh and unconstrained, before he came up against such pragmatic challenges as developing a workable, structured teaching programme in rural England, say, or was trying in practice to get such complexities across to actors from different parts of the world, or having to make concessions in his writings to meet the demands of American editors.[27] Now that a series of explorations known as the Chekhov Technique has been available to actors for some time, it is easy to lose sight of the Herculean task that it was to create the form and imagery capable of allowing us to follow Chekhov's path as an artist. The 'Paris Manuscript' bears witness to this and reminds us that the work itself transcends by far the sum of a series of exercises. It was also the only text about acting that was written while Chekhov was still fully active as a stage artist and regularly creating and performing characters, and even in rough draft he is always distinct and very often eloquent.[28]

Readers may also come to share the view that the 'Paris Manuscript' solicits a cross-examination of a few of the tendencies that Andrei Kirillov was clearly already picking up on in 2005 (see the Preface in this book), and that have continued to gain traction in some assessments of Chekhov's life and work. Reading between the lines of some commentators – and in one or two instances, right on the lines – we find a narrative portraying his so-called 'ideology' as fundamentally quixotic or utopian, very much the 'outdated fantasy of that gentleman alone', as Kirillov puts it,[29] with the broader and deeper quest beyond the prevalent canon of his acting exercises – a philosophy often but variously identified as his 'Theatre of the Future' – deemed to have been a failed experiment, or interpreted as a never realized prophesy. Such appraisals are often convincingly argued and may make compelling reading, but are certainly not the whole truth regarding so much of what Chekhov develops in the 'Paris Manuscript' and beyond. Nor would such judgements be corroborated by our own experience at the studio and, I believe, that of a great many artists and teachers around the world exploring this work in practice.[30] A troubling aspect of diminishing, dismissing or in some sense overlooking the distinction of Chekhov's far-reaching spiritual or metaphysical vision is surely the long-term danger that his legacy be to a consequential degree reduced or simplified, that what ultimately endures is not his holistic invitation to investigate and develop oneself, but a series of self-contained, results-based practices, either because actors learn and apply dutifully versions of a few quickly accessible exercises in certain given situations they have been taught, or because, as is so often the case, teachers and artists are forced to make difficult choices merely to suit the existing structures and time constraints of teaching or rehearsal programmes, online media, and our *Zeitgeist* generally, rather than actual creative needs or possibilities.

Any serious-minded individual artist or group, meanwhile, with the time, curiosity, patience and indeed vocation to penetrate for themselves what it is to be an artist, rather than see exercises as a template for achieving fixed or pre-conceived results, would be unlikely to share such views about Chekhov's underlying philosophy and emphasis on individual development. We would argue – on the evidence of the 'Paris Manuscript' alone – that Chekhov was far more a visionary than utopian, the distinction here being that a utopian's imagined world will be ruled to have been inherently impractical, hence experimental and doomed from the outset, so in some sense a lapse on their part. Whereas if a visionary's better world never materialized, or hasn't yet, or not fully, then this is evidently the failing of others, and often the community as a whole. To take an analogy from another corner of society, we wouldn't label Martin Luther King Jr's famous 1963 'I have a dream' speech a quixotic, outdated fantasy or failed utopian vision, simply because the systemic racial inequality in the United States and elsewhere around the world still persists so vigorously.

The fact that Chekhov's vision has sometimes been portrayed as experimental or overly 'spiritual' (implying that this side of his legacy needn't be taken too seriously or that it is impractical) is surely not because the ideology behind the work he developed as an actor, director and teacher was in any way unsound, naïve or utopian and may therefore be reasonably skimmed over, but proof, if further proof were needed, that the world has very much been swept up in the tsunami of dry intellectual thinking that Chekhov himself could already see gathering pace, to the point where such ideas now appear (at least to many) utopian or even foolish. Chekhov is hardly alone here, and Joseph Beuys immediately springs to mind as another example of a sage with a kindred worldview and sense of foreboding, whose legacy was in his time (and is to this day) often dismissed as impenetrable or simply irrelevant. And while it is doubtless true that it hasn't in any critical sense become a dominant influence in the world – so a failed experiment? – Beuys's ambitious vision of the transformative force of individual creativity as part of a social organism seems nevertheless prescient (and indeed may – like Chekhov's – be as relevant and urgent as ever). Throughout history society has marginalized such admonitions at its peril, and while there is no question that Chekhov experimented and that he failed many times, this was no more than one would expect to come with the territory of any great artist's trajectory, and certainly such a turbulent one as his. Let us be clear: Samuel Beckett's famous line in *Worstward Ho*, 'Ever tried. Ever failed. No matter. Try again. Fail again. Fail better.'[31] should be taken as a cry of <u>encouragement</u>, something for artists everywhere to embrace and live by.

Our own experience at the studio has been that, taken as a whole, what Chekhov writes here and develops later regarding the so-called spiritual aspects of creativity and the future challenges for actors, is in no sense outdated, unsound, failed or experimental, and that all of it can and perhaps even should be of <u>practical</u> relevance to artists generally. It is, after all, nothing other than an inspired subjective vision of the 'ground rules of human creativity' [77] within the context of a society whose form and direction of travel can so hinder us that the very paths of artistic creation start to feel utterly counter-intuitive, and become far easier (and quicker) to dismiss than to trust. In this early work, the philosophical and meditative aspects of what it is to be an artist are given freer rein than in much of Chekhov's later output, or than one might expect to encounter in a great many acting workshops nowadays. There are no specific exercises in the 'Paris Manuscript' for creating character, say, or for working with objectives and other more obviously practical 'acting tools', and even the exercises in the missing annex would appear, as far as one can deduce from the context in which they are mentioned in the main text, to be for strengthening the artist's concentration, imagination, sense of space and inner life generally (in other words, the formation of the 'iceberg' rather than 'tools'). Also, although we know the early 1930s to have been a period of experimentation with theatrical form, neither does Chekhov present us here with some sort of unusual vision of theatre. Instead, he simply brings together the many characteristics of humankind's creative process as it relates to acting, and presents elements to which actors (and indeed artists generally) should pay particular attention, not only to protect themselves from being swept up unwittingly in the encroaching materialization and mechanization of society, but to lucidly make the most of all that the future will bring.

Now that nearly a century has elapsed since Chekhov and Boner were working through these ideas together, some observations actually seem prescient.

> [Matter] will intrude more and more on people's lives, and the more people become dependent on the now-moving matter, the more life will start to resemble a mechanism. The moving matter, the mechanism will work like a spell on people, and this spellbinding power will develop because the more complete the mechanism, the more it will resemble the human intellect. A powerful intellect that has become mechanistic in the service of human beings will influence humans like a magic spell. The sense of awe of the mechanistic will cost humankind dearly.

Surely I am not alone in perceiving in these lines [64] the distant magnetic lure of the smartphone, the all-pervading internet and even our twenty-first century concerns about AI, and I also clearly sense in the following observation the imminent shallow rush of the world of social media [55]:

> An opinion will always remain superficial, without roots. And just as a consistent *Weltanschauung* harmonizes human thinking, feeling, and willing, a mere opinion will disrupt these three forces. (Or rather, a host of opinions: an opinion can never be alone since contrary opinions will always follow in droves).

So perhaps there are still messages to be found within these pages of the never completed 'Paris Manuscript', if only we are able to engage with it simply, personally, seeking what it might mean for our practice, both as artists and more broadly as fellow actors, directors and teachers guiding others. Occasionally, whenever I have succeeded in setting aside all the busy knowledge I have about Chekhov's fascinating later life, the canon of other writings and all the scholarship that has taken place since his death, I have had the fleeting sense of being the third presence in the Chekhovs' rented house in Riga, or out in their garden, or walking in the nearby fields a few steps behind Misha and Georgette as they wrestle with how on earth to write about something so personal and intangible and numinous as the actor's creative process – how to express it in language, where to start, what will people understand? I suspect I'd have been the rather more sceptical of the group, slow to pick up on the fact that my dear friends were on to something astounding that would surely resonate for generations.

Perhaps one lesson that may still be taken from the 'Paris Manuscript' is the reminder that serious, viable paths will always exist beyond our traditionally hierarchical structures. From this early attempt at writing about the actor's craft through to all that he shared with the many actors who went to study under him in Hollywood in the 1950s and for whom he became an artistic mentor, Michael Chekhov consistently presents all that he develops as a source of investigation and personal growth, never as a template, and he respectfully deserves to always be listened to and followed in that light.

Editing and Abridging Chekhov's Text

The 'Paris Manuscript' abandoned by Chekhov and Boner in late 1934 would still have required a great deal of work before it might conceivably have been published (I think we may presume that at the time this was generally the intention), and I have therefore undertaken the critical editing and revision work required to bring a large part of it into a presentable form, while at all times taking care to remain on this side of the boundary between editor/translator and co-author. So although the entire manuscript has been carefully worked through and at times abridged, the result should nevertheless be recognized as an early draft text and read in that spirit.[32] The work published here represents about two-thirds of the complete text in the Zurich archive, with the largest single cuts coming from sections dealing with speech and rhythm that include lengthy examples in German; their laborious recreation in English would have required overstepping in no small measure my role as editor/translator (and the resulting version in any case been of doubtful practical use to actors).[33]

The translation work itself has allowed for a general tidying up of the remaining text and the natural elimination of an assortment of minor lapses, while some repetition or revisiting of themes (particularly in the second half of the book) has also been addressed, either with further cuts or at times through some form

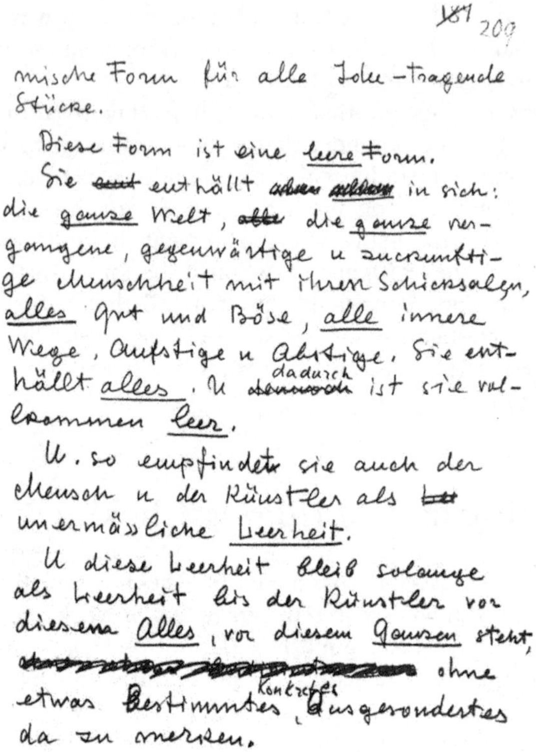

FIGURE 14 Page 209 of the 'Paris Manuscript'.

of consolidation. Once or twice I ended up playing secretary, so for instance where Chekhov left the parenthetical note: 'Goethe's phrase about the exact imagination.', this has been replaced by the lines by Goethe to which he makes reference.[34] However, the cuts and other alterations notwithstanding, my overall approach has been to remain light-handed as editor, so that readers may feel as close as possible to the handwritten text of the notebooks and make their own discoveries and critical interpretations among these pages. Chekhov's idiosyncratic underlining marks and occasional use of upper case emphasis have therefore all been maintained, but the side notes to Boner and references to the missing annex of exercises have been eliminated, as have the pagination markings, of which there are a great many and evidence of how frequently the running order of most sections was amended (at least four times). I too was tempted to alter the order here and there and make further 'improvements', but not being able to consult either the author or his collaborator, felt for the most part that this would be trespassing beyond the task in hand. Chekhov's division of the text into paragraphs was irregular, so these have been revised throughout, and some section divisions were reinforced for the sake of clarity. Here, though, I at least had a noble precedent in the form of Deirdre Hurst du Prey, who always provided helpful markers in all her transcriptions of Chekhov's classes and lectures. The subheadings found throughout the text, meanwhile, are all directly from the original manuscript (where they appear framed in the page margins).

Now, since neither Chekhov nor Boner is with us to have their say in any of this, I am acutely aware that all the choices about the final text presented here – indeed the decision to put this book forward for publication at all – have been entirely subjective and mine alone. I can only hope they would find them to be respectful and generally approve. The only justifications I can proffer for assuming this great responsibility are the fountain of experience that Thaís Loureiro and I cherished so lovingly in the years we had working together at the studio we founded, and that our small community of actors has continued to help nurture ever since; my eagerness to share what I consider to be a precious and still highly relevant and indeed timely document for practising artists; and also the warm encouragement and support I received from Prof. Anton Rey (ZHdK) and others throughout the research and creation of this book.

Translating Chekhov's German

As has already been touched upon, among the benefits Chekhov enjoyed writing in German was the clarity that language affords generally, but particularly by two adjectives for which there is no accurate equivalent in English, *seelisch* and *geistig*. Our word 'spiritual' comes close but is vague by comparison, and in any case we rarely use that word in the context of our acting work because in the classroom or rehearsal space it will generally raise a few eyebrows or feel uneasy, even when qualified first in order to deflect any religious connotations. So in referring to the incorporeal part of the human experience that is so central to our creative work, we commonly end up reaching for expressions such as 'energy body', 'inner life' and 'inwardly', 'the heart', 'presence', 'living spirit' and 'invisible body' (the last two occasionally used by Chekhov himself in English), or simply resort to whole phrases in order to refer to what is certainly a complex and – crucially – full-bodied cognitive world.

We also have the well-trodden term 'psycho-physical', and as Chekhov became more settled into English (from 1936) he frequently adopted 'psychology' and 'psychological' to cover this ground of our incorporeal experience, albeit somewhat loosely.[35] But in both these instances the prefix 'psycho' would appear to have been given the task of single-handedly representing the entire non-physical portion of our existence. The term does of course derive from the Greek *psykhē*, which refers to the soul, mind and even spirit, but nowadays most dictionaries will define 'psycho' as some variation of 'relating to the mind or psychology',[36] hence sending us intuitively towards our mental state. In the acting world we also frequently see 'mind' being juxtaposed with 'body', and here again, our English language appears to cater far more readily to only one portion of our intangible human experience, the head/mind.

For actors, however, the full-bodied part of our incorporeal life that lies beyond, or to be quite literal, below the world of the mind is certainly of great, if not greater significance, so it is somewhat unfortunate that our language lets us down in this way. Chekhov recognized and constantly drew a clear distinction between the nature of the inner life of our mind on the one hand, and that of our torso, limbs and lower body on the other,[37] and it is precisely this distinction that he was able to make with such ease when writing in German, for not only do *seelisch* and *geistig* cover between them the entirety of the human cognitive world, from incorporeal head to toe, so to speak, but they differentiate between our dual experience of it. Furthermore, both words may conveniently be employed as adjectives or adverbs, and for good measure each is directly related to a noun (*Seele* and *Geist*), while neither is likely to raise eyebrows among German speaking actors, referring as they do to two spheres of our <u>lived, worldly</u> experience of the spiritual, something Chekhov would later refer to as the actor's 'intangible means of expression'.[38]

Now, having presented the fluency and clarity Chekhov enjoyed writing in the German language as one of the chief points of interest in this early text, it clearly makes no sense for this effectiveness to now be lost in my translation. And so, in the spirit of Robert Frost's famous line 'I can see no way out but through',[39] readers will find that *seelisch/Seele* and *geistig/Geist* have been simply left as Chekhov wrote them, italicized throughout, along with a couple of other key words that in the context of his specific usage also present translation issues. Of course, this does mean that we will have to take a moment to go over them together, but for actors and artists eager to get the most out of Chekhov's vision as presented here for your practice, the modest effort required to break out of the confines of English in order to grasp these expressions will, at least on the evidence of our own discoveries at the studio, be immediately eclipsed by the insights emerging from the clearer comprehension of so much of what he develops here (and indeed later). The other terms that have been left in German are *Gestalt* and *Weltanschauung/Weltempfindung*; in each case, there is a fundamental conceptual reason that makes this the right choice for a translation of the 'Paris Manuscript' as a sourcebook, as we shall now see.

Seelisch, geistig

We have already mentioned that these words might reasonably be translated as 'spiritual', the translation very often given for both,[40] but although German–English dictionaries will reveal the overlap, it should be noted that German does have its own word *spirituell* (indeed it appears in the 'Paris Manuscript' and has been translated without further ado), whereas *seelisch* and *geistig* are quite distinct. In German texts generally the precise meaning can sometimes vary a little, but Chekhov's usage is clear and may be illustrated by a Venn diagram in which our incorporeal life is represented by two overlapping circles, one covering *geistig* and the noun *Geist*, and the other *seelisch* and *Seele* (Figure 15). The intersection would indeed give us the shared dictionary definition of 'spiritual/spirit', but *geistig* refers particularly to the higher world of ideas, dreams, our thinking, memory, our imagination and connection to the universe, as well as our psychology and the intellect. In the present context, *Geist* would most commonly be translated as 'mind'.

Seelisch, on the other hand, is suggestive of our temporal lived experience of the world around us, from the neck down, as it were: our inner movement that accompanies the rich life of our sensations, feelings and emotions, with their qualities, rhythms, expansions and contractions, our connection with and responses to the physical world, as well as the mighty, ever-dependable vigour of our lower body that is so clearly present in our experience of the will. The most common English translation of the corresponding noun *Seele* is 'soul', but it is mostly used by Chekhov here in the sense of our inner life generally (and again, as quite distinct from our mind). Now, as you move through the 'Paris Manuscript', you will right from the very first lines have the opportunity to grow familiar with this pair of words, and the clarity they afford within the context of our practical work and what Chekhov was expressing so precisely will, I believe, be readily apparent. To give just two quick examples: in the book's opening lines he refers to the exercises as being '*seelisch*-physical' [28], which, as can easily be guessed, would otherwise have ended up in translation as 'psycho-physical'. However, since Chekhov is referring here expressly to something other than the mind, that translation choice would have been a real distraction. He also refers more than once to the triad of our 'physical, *seelisch* and *geistig* human traits' [52]. These would likely have become the simplified (and vague): 'physical and spiritual human traits'; or perhaps, were one to follow the example of his later texts in English, 'physical and psychological human traits', thereby drifting even further from the original sense. Whereas having now received these German expressions, readers may follow with clarity Chekhov's original intentions for themselves.

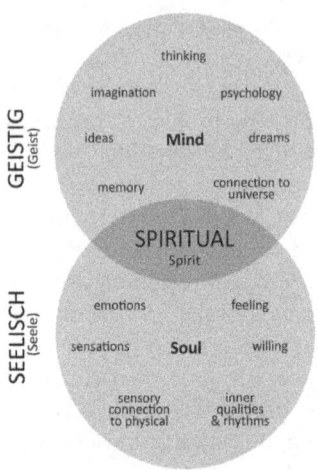

FIGURE 15 *Venn diagram: seelisch vs. geistig elements of the human experience. Illustration by Beatrice Moss. Michael Chekhov Brasil archive*

In abstract analytical terms such shades of meaning may appear trivial or perhaps even fussy, but as soon as actors come to our explorations in practice we quickly find that *seelisch* and *geistig* are indeed whole worlds apart, and that so much of what Chekhov is able to express here will certainly radiate back into our creative work as soon as we return to the studio or rehearsal space.

Gestalt (plural *Gestalten*)

Depending on the context, *Gestalt* might variously be translated throughout this text as 'form', 'shape', 'object', 'figure', 'entity', 'being', 'person', 'character' (all of these preceded in many instances by the adjective 'imaginary') or simply as 'image'. Unlike *seelisch/geistig* there is no translation problem here as such, since all these choices are perfectly good ones. No, I have opted to leave *Gestalt* well alone precisely <u>because</u> Chekhov uses it in such a range of disparate situations right across the arc of artistic creation, and it is vital that actors and artists studying this text not be deprived of something that, again, when it comes to our practice, goes far beyond some erudite semantic point.

In his use of *Gestalt* to refer to everything from physical forms (including people) in a space, to actual or imaginary objects in a concentration exercise, to the random images which visit our imaginations as we fall asleep and in our dreams, or the specific characters in plays that we picture in our mind's eye or that can be seen on stage, with their outer/physical and inner/spiritual lives, and that actors become one with in the final stage of a creative process, Chekhov is able to emphasize something profound about the unified, cohesive way in which we are not only able to perceive both the physical and imagined universe, but should actively be encouraged to do so (and indeed train). This harks back to Goethe's concept of an 'exact sensorial imagination'[41] that Chekhov makes reference to here [66] and elsewhere, the notion that the imagination must be seen as a legitimate and reliable cognitive organ that must be put to <u>practical</u> use.

Weltanschauung and *Weltempfindung*

The word *Weltanschauung* is not entirely foreign to English readers, being usually understood as akin to a philosophy of life. Whenever it is translated, it becomes the English 'worldview', but while the first part of the compound word does of course mean 'world', in the present context 'view' is not such a good reflection of *Anschauung*, since it is being used by Chekhov more in the sense of an ongoing 'perception' or 'perspective', and he specifically describes how an actor's ever increasing perception of the complex environment all around continually forms their *Welt/Anschauung*, something that also shapes and is shaped by our individuality and the forces of our thinking, feeling, willing.

This is incredibly important because, as you will see, Chekhov's *Weltanschauung* is more a creative organ of perception in constant development and interaction with the world (also the world of a play) – a conscious or subconscious 'everyday relationship to the world' – rather than the intellectual, more passive or static philosophy or cultural outlook on life likely suggested by 'worldview'. Chekhov then builds on this idea further by introducing the notion of *Weltempfindung*, which is not a common word in German but unambiguous in meaning. *Empfindung* means 'feeling', so the literal translation here would be: 'world-feeling'. *Weltempfindung* also emphasizes the constant flow of how we feel and sense the world, and again, rather than place myself between readers and Chekhov the author, I prefer to allow you to acquire from the context your own intuitive sense of and familiarity with his precise expressions.

Work/work and Idea/idea

These two words present no translation issues as such, but just for clarity's sake, the word 'work' has taken the sentence case in the many instances that refer to an overall composition, rather than the activity of labour. For an example of why this is important to distinguish, we find Chekhov talking about 'the author's Work' (in German, *Werk*), while a few paragraphs later he refers to 'the upcoming work by the actors' (*Arbeit*).

Similarly, 'Idea' has been used to indicate an idea in the sense of backbone or central concept, as opposed to notion or thought. For instance, Chekhov writes *Autorenidee* and *Idee des Stückes*, giving us: 'author's Idea' and 'play's Idea', respectively, as opposed to the meaning in a phrase like: 'Whenever artists are seized by a creative idea'.

A final note on the language

Although the adjectives *seelisch* and *geistig* have been left in the original, they have out of necessity been excused here of the declensions that the rules of German grammar demand of them. In other words, they behave like English adjectives throughout, giving us a '*seelisch* atmosphere' and a '*geistig* being', rather than '*seelische*' and '*geistiges*', respectively. For any readers who do speak German, these phrasings will certainly jar somewhat, so I both appeal to and thank you in advance for your patience and goodwill.

A Memo to the Reader

When I take my ten-month-old granddaughter Bella out in her pushchair, I've noticed that she has two modes of delight in and fascination for all that we come across: Soft Bella rests, leaning comfortably back, observing all around attentively but somewhat passively and, as I imagine it, receiving the world flowing towards her on curved lines; while Hunter Bella sits bolt upright, eyes and head darting around, eagerly seeking the next point of interest, fully active and constantly grasping the world rushing towards her along straight lines.

Soft Bella would get a lot more out of the 'Paris Manuscript' than readers who 'go at' this text hunting for things to do, clear paths and exercises, or than those impatient to fold this ur-text into their analysis and previous judgements of Chekhov. Indeed, Hunter Bella may even be disappointed and deem this early work to be of limited interest after all, frustrated by its unfinished and somewhat rough state that has resulted, among other things, in an abrupt opening (as has already been noted, among the missing pages are precisely the book's foreword).[42] So my advice would be to initially not do very much beyond simply absorbing what Chekhov is saying, allowing the ideas to flow through and around you and speak to your individual experience of being an actor and artist (his declared intended readership), before gradually imagining how it all might be relevant to your practice today. Again, what follows is an early draft text, and since the running order of the sections was very likely still a work in progress, dipping in and out according to whim may well provide as much enjoyment as a logical working through in the sequence in which these pages were left behind in Paris all those decades ago.

One undeniable thrill that we get from delving into the 'Paris Manuscript' in the Zurich archive is that, despite being only a photocopy (except for two diagrams that are the original pages), we are constantly aware that the text is in Michael Chekhov's own hand, and a dozen facsimile pages have been included here so that readers may sense the immediacy of the man himself, as well as follow some of the frantic revision marks and pagination alterations littering the entire draft.

Now, as you read on, gladly accept the invitation to slow down and be Soft Bella.

The 'Paris Manuscript'

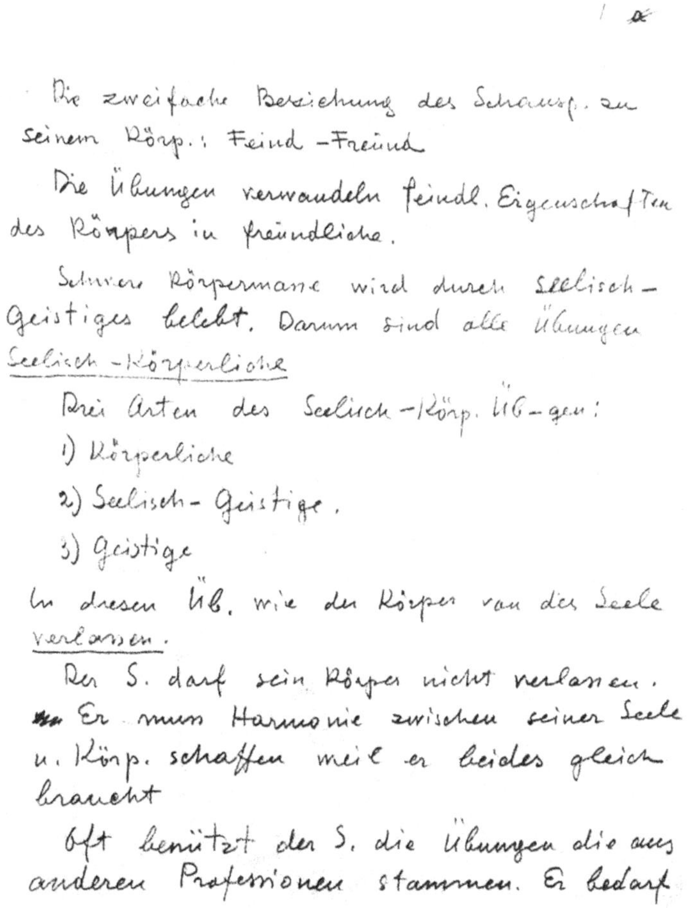

Die zweifache Beziehung des Schausp. zu seinem Körp.: Feind – Freund

Die Übungen verwandeln feindl. Eigenschaften des Körpers in freundliche.

Schwere Körpermasse wird durch Seelisch-Geistiges belebt. Darum sind alle Übungen Seelisch-Körperliche

Drei Arten des Seelisch-Körp. Üb-gen:
1) Körperliche
2) Seelisch- Geistige.
3) Geistige

In diesen Üb. wie der Körper von der Seele verlassen.

Der S. darf sein Körper nicht verlassen. Er muss Harmonie zwischen seiner Seele u. Körp. schaffen weil er beides gleich braucht

Oft benützt der S. die Übungen die aus anderen Professionen stammen. Er bedarf

FIGURE 16 *The first surviving page of the 'Paris Manuscript'.*

Attention

Actors have a twofold relationship with their body: Enemy – Friend. Exercises can turn the body's hostile traits into allies. Heavy body mass is stimulated by all that is *seelisch-geistig*. So the exercises are *seelisch*-physical. They fall into three types:

1) Physical
2) *Seelisch-geistig*
3) *Geistig*

Through such exercises the *Seele* can become free, but actors cannot escape their body and since both are needed, harmony must be created between the two. Actors often use exercises that stem from other professions, yet we also need exercises that derive from the idea of the actor's art, in other words: the body's permeability for all that is *seelisch-geistig*. This distinguishes the actor's profession from all others that also employ the body. Actors' bodies require not only a particular development through pure acting exercises, but speech must also be expressly trained and developed through special exercises, and our imaginational skills must also be developed and perfected.

These three fields of the acting technique, when properly developed, can be described as a general acting technique. We might illustrate the human body that isn't yet developed as heavy and flat on the ground; similarly, if we were to present our weak, static ability to imagine and our inartistically formed use of human speech in a diagram, we might trace a horizontal line along the ground. Then everything that emerges as a new skill in the actor's body, the speech and the activity of the imagination, these could be shown on our diagram as a vertical line. Certain physical and *seelisch* powers will be lifted from the earth, so to speak, and raised up. Actors can achieve this rising up with a general acting technique. (Figure I)

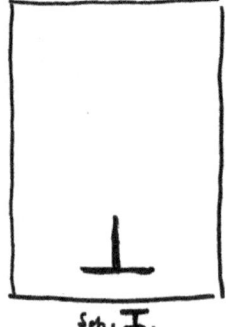

Sch. I.

There is also a special technique that every actor must devise and create afresh for each role, based on the general technique. Now, before we come to the development of the general acting technique, we must speak of a particular trait. Actors must first develop this trait within themselves, because without it they cannot carry out the exercises correctly and productively. In fact, the entire creative process depends on this trait. Actors require a particular kind of <u>attention</u>. The development of this attention must be built upon our everyday ability to concentrate, so to begin with, a series of standard, well-known concentration exercises must be practiced.

The distinctive feature of this attention will be developed by gradually learning to connect and unify our *Seele*, our <u>whole being</u>, with an object; by trying to follow the life of the object not just with our eyes and ears, but with <u>inner warm-heartedness</u>. For instance, we concentrate on an object and then make an inner effort to, so to speak, <u>penetrate</u> the object with the full power of our *Seele*, as if sending part of our being to the object and allowing it to work on us. We offer up, as it were, our *seelisch* being to the object. Then, through a sort of <u>love</u>, we connect to the object.

Through this trait, this type of attention on the part of actors, all the exercises we undertake will always seem <u>new</u>, as if <u>for the first time</u>. The *seelisch* warmth that actors sustain throughout these exercises will gradually reveal all their secrets and they will be deepened, their effect become strong and successful. In order to attain this particular attention we must try and find this connection with <u>every</u> object.

There is another, second trait that actors must develop within themselves. It is a direct consequence of the first, is organically linked to it, and is gradually achieved by connecting to an object until we find ourselves loving the object, as described above. Then, once this state is reached, we try to develop an inner activity of considering the object's properties, the forces working on it, the processes acting on it. This is a process of <u>feeling for</u>. We feel ourselves in the object and we <u>feel for</u> it with our *seelisch* powers. So this feeling for is to actually experience it.

Let us take an example. We immerse ourselves in a stone. We begin by thinking about its properties – in other words, we inwardly feel for these properties. We feel for the stone's <u>heaviness</u> – so that we <u>experience</u> the stone's heaviness. We feel for, therefore we experience, the stone's <u>opacity</u>, etc. Or to take another example: before us is a human *Gestalt* that we've created in our imagination. We concentrate on this imaginary *Gestalt* just as we concentrated on the stone. We send out our *seelisch* powers to our *Gestalt* and penetrate it lovingly with these powers. And just as with the stone, we begin to get a *seelisch* feel for the *Gestalt*. We recognize in our <u>experience</u> its *seelisch* traits, its physical forms, its feelings etc.

And a further example, an abstract idea such as: 'Every action has an effect.' As an abstract idea we cannot get a feeling for it, so we need to turn it into an image, for instance we might imagine the 'action' as a power current, a streaming wave, a colourful ray, something like that. Then we might imagine the 'effect' as some form or colour gathering strength, or as an increasingly dense substance etc. The main point being that we have turned an abstract idea into an <u>image</u>, and once we have that before us, we can direct our attention towards this image in the described manner and connect to it with our *seelisch* powers, just as we did with the stone or the imaginary person. There is <u>no</u> object that <u>cannot</u> be observed in this way.

Actors should also practice these two important traits, this particular type of attention, together. This is most important. Through such exercises great *seelisch* forces will unfold within us, something we need for our work, which is always <u>collective</u>. These powers provide actors with the wonderful possibility of unifying inwardly within a truthful ensemble, in the highest and best sense of the word. The quality of the actor's imagination will also be increased by training this ability to feel for something inwardly at will, and it will become more profound and precise. The images will no longer be experienced as something unclear or vague in the imagination, but rather they will become perfectly clear and absolutely concrete.

Whenever artists are seized by a creative idea, it can happen that they simply begin, through their increased life force, to inwardly start feeling for it. However, such happy moments in life and in an artist's work are infrequent. This was more common in earlier times, but nowadays such fiery moments are rare and only arrive by chance. Today's artists can no longer take the liberty of <u>only waiting for</u> moments of inspiration for our creative work. We must develop in ourselves that which artists frequently used to have as a gift. This is an important difference between the artists of yesterday and today. In previous times, inspiration was the <u>outset of a creation</u>; now it can be understood as the <u>conclusion of our work</u>.

In other words, artists today must develop their inspiration and then place their trust in the creative *Geist*. This is difficult, but it is beneficial. Why? Because for the artist of tomorrow, inspiration will be a free act of the will. Inspiration will be voluntarily called upon, but only if the artists of today apply their forces to this inner work. This attention and inner feeling for things are the powers that will lead to inspiration.

Movement

Now let us delve into the rich and wonderful field of artistic movement.

Aesthetic joy

One thing that must be said is that human beings have been richly gifted and endowed – by Nature's creative forces – with the possibility of movement. As artists, actors adopt their own bodies and the ability to move as a means of expression, and must develop a particularly refined sensibility towards movement. This consists of becoming aware, through appropriate exercises, of an aesthetic feeling, an aesthetic joy associated to each movement. Every living being that has been granted the gift of the ability to move, experiences in their movement a certain joy. Such is the gift of Nature.

Because of the way we live nowadays, this natural joy in each movement has disappeared from our consciousness. Now we only notice our physical movements whenever the body is sick and it aches when we move. But artists, and particularly actors, must quite consciously revitalise this natural joy. Artists must take constant pleasure in their moving instrument. All our movements will be received by the audience as artistic if they are performed with aesthetic joy.

Actors can nurture this by developing within themselves a feeling for broad, artistic and free movements. This feeling causes everything that is desperate, petty or tight, to disappear. Life today no longer knows such free and artistically beautiful movements, with actors' everyday habits being carried over onto the stage and spoiling their gestures. Nowadays, in plays performed with naturalism, we no longer even notice when actors adopt habitual, everyday inartistic gestures. Through this feeling for broad and complete movements, and provided they aren't forced into portraying the character with desperate, small movements, actors will give audiences a clear artistic impression.

There is another feeling that actors must carefully train in order to be able to experience the whole body as a work of art, a valuable instrument at their disposal in their work. Three main forces of the human *Seele* are also elements of the art of acting, requiring a particular permeability of the body in order to manifest themselves. These elements are: thinking, feeling, willing. The first is most beautifully expressed through floating, the second through radiating and the third through moulding gestures. However this does not mean that actors, while working on stage, or while rehearsing, should think about which gestures they should choose for different sections of their part. It is just a question of actors having at their disposal these three types of movement. Their artistic instinct, their artistic intuition alone will choose and use these previously trained gestures. Floating, radiating and moulding gestures must live in the actor's *Seele* and in their body as abilities, not as laws that will limit the actor's freedom.

A clear, definite, self-contained, complete gesture plays an important role on stage. We often see how actors are unable to express their clearly formed inner life, simply because their gestures lapse into something vague, formless. They will often seek to express this inner life through several gestures, rather than applying one well formed self-contained gesture. The habit of being able to express each *seelisch* movement clearly and completely through outer physical movement, must reside within the body itself.

The actor's *Seele* must be in no doubt as to whether their inner life will find expression in their body. And in turn, the body's artistic habit of self-contained, complete gestures will work on the actor's *Seele*, thereby helping find inner *seelisch* forms as self-contained, complete gestures, and awakening in us a love for this type of well constructed inner experience.

The body defines imaginary forms

The actor's body has a great influence on the forms they imagine. Actors are usually aware to some degree of their bodies' artistic possibilities. They know roughly to what degree their bodies are agile, light, expressively precise, skilful etc., and this instinctive knowledge will also shape an actor's imagination as they work on a part. If their body isn't agile and doesn't have this lightness, they will instinctively imagine the *Gestalt* of their part in heavy physical and *seelisch* images. So the development of the body is at the same time the development of the imagination and an actor's imaginary activity will be less hampered by a developed body than an undeveloped one. Therefore all correctly crafted physical exercises must also be considered exercises for the *Seele*.

There is another *seelisch*-physical trait that actors must develop within themselves, and it is this: a <u>confident and light handling</u>

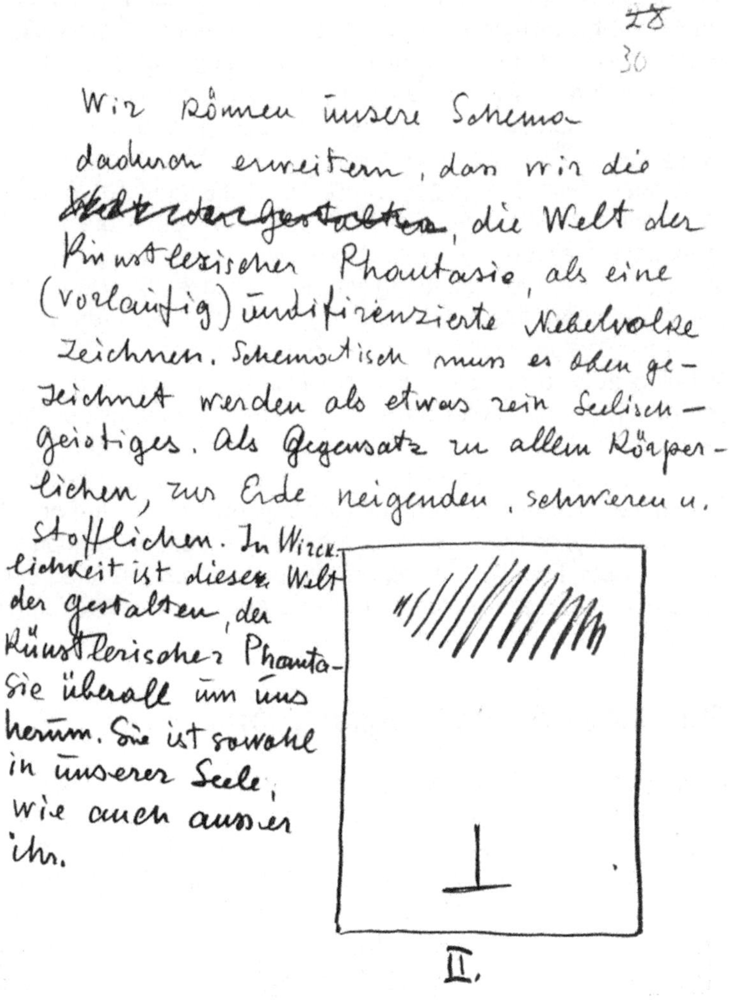

> 28
> 30
>
> Wir können unsere Schema dadurch erweitern, dass wir die ~~Welt der Gestalten~~, die Welt der Künstlerischen Phantasie, als eine (vorläufig) undifirenzierte Nebelwolke zeichnen. Schematisch muss es eben gezeichnet werden als etwas rein Seelisch-Geistiges. Als Gegensatz zu allem Körperlichen, zur Erde neigenden, schweren u. Stofflichen. In Wirklichkeit ist dieser Welt der Gestalten, der Künstlerischer Phantasie überall um uns herum. Sie ist sowohl in unserer Seele, wie auch ausser ihr.
>
> II.

FIGURE 17 *Page 30 of the 'Paris Manuscript'.*

of their body. Again, this skilfulness, agility and lightness of the body is only one aspect of becoming confident, light on stage, because in order to achieve this the actor's *Seele* must also be confident. This confidence has nothing to do with overrating oneself or stage chutzpah. A true, noble confidence permeated with aesthetic feelings is an appealing trait in an actor. Everything that hides behind a mask of 'confidence', however, creates an unsympathetic atmosphere and offends the audience.

The borderline between confidence and 'confidence' is so thin that while we work we must take care to maintain the correct one. This remark isn't given out of a lack of trust in those working, but rather because our own bodies have themselves the constant tendency, as soon as they are able to be free and confident, to suddenly become rather bold. This has to do with contemporary life, in which our bodies constantly feel rather inhibited and restrained by pressure from our intellect, not being an artistic element of our *Seele*.

Changeable space

The space on stage is a special space, a complex space. The scenery divides and carves up the space in a variety of ways. Each set is its own spatial world. Actors fill this space with their bodies, they complement it. Each set makes certain demands on actors, and in order to meet these demands actors must be able to develop an inner feeling that gives them the possibility to physically move easily around the set. One can develop a refined inner sense of space through certain exercises.

As soon as a human *Gestalt* steps into the space of a set, it is already quite a different space. A living human *Gestalt* alters the arrangement of the space. For instance, a pillar with someone standing beside it presents a completely different spatial form to one with no one there. All scenic spatial circumstances change through the presence of actors on stage and each new arrival finds a set altered by the scene partners. We must be able to get our bearings in the space in order to move artistically and with rhythm.

Now, because actors on stage must move within the given set, it means the spatial circumstances are also flexible. If the actors' sense is that the scenery is a rigid, unchanging form, it will be artistically false. If with the movement of our scene partners, we sense no spatial <u>change</u>, it is because our spatial sense isn't yet sufficiently sensitive. In our ordinary, everyday lives, we have no aesthetic, artistic spatial sense. Life today is under the influence of the cold intellect, which is what guides us, and because it is no 'artist', nor is life today an 'aesthetic' life. But this cold inartistic tendency of the intellect can be carried onto the stage in the form of naturalism. The deadening power of the intellect expresses itself in the field of stagecraft in various ways, and because the tendencies of the everyday intellectual consciousness and our artistic consciousness are in opposition, both cannot exist on stage <u>at the same time</u>. There is either the <u>usefulness</u> of the intellect, or the <u>beauty</u> of art.

The actor's ability to be guided by a flexible and living stage space is to create that which is beautiful. The important matter of the *mise-en-scène* will be perfectly resolved if actors develop within themselves a refined spatial sense. Directors who strive for a complete composition and harmony will be better able to fulfil this task if they have at their disposal a group of actors who nurture this spatial sense through patient, careful work.

Imagination

We now turn to the field of the imagination from the point of view of the general acting technique.

Every human being is endowed by nature with the ability to imagine. Every human being is surrounded by a whole world of moving, flowing *Gestalten*. Every human being dreams not only during sleep, but also in a state of wakefulness. Nowadays such *Gestalten* don't penetrate most people's consciousness, for the impressions of outer life are so strong and coarse that they suppress the fine, delicate and flowing *Gestalten* of the imagination. These *Gestalten* are thrust into the unconscious regions of the life of our *Seele*.

Artists, actors, however, must have this world of *Gestalten* in their clear daytime consciousness, being the material from which they must create their works. Artists first transform an artistic idea through the activity of the imagination into an image that is only later embodied on stage. The ability to imagine can, like any human ability, be increased and developed through suitable practice. One often hears actors claim they aren't able to see the *Gestalten* clearly enough, and are therefore obliged to work in more intellectual ways, less through the inspiration of the imagination. To this we must respond that it is not a matter of the *Gestalten* being absent, but rather an inability to notice and hold them in one's consciousness. What is lacking here is the organ of awareness, so to speak, of the world of the imagination, but not this world as such.

Before actors can begin to develop this organ, we must find the correct relationship to the world of the imagination. Many great artists of the past and the present day have spoken about this relationship, always stressing, in different ways and from different points of view, that the world of the imagination is in a sense an independent world, even that they cannot credit their Work only and exclusively to themselves. The world of the imagination bestows us with its gifts, with *Gestalten*, sounds, rhythms etc. The artist's imagination is a definite inner activity on the part of the artist's self and at the same time it is also the activity of our world of *Gestalten*. Guided by this truth, which great artists down through the ages have known, artists and actors can form the correct and most beautiful relationship with the world of the imagination.

It is destructive and paralysing for an artist to think they are the lone creator in the sphere of the imagination. This thought causes the *Seele* to close in on itself and puts too much of a demand on the artist, while the world of the imagination also closes in on itself and will offer them no gifts. The result is that in a certain (and subtle) sense they end up falling into a type of artistic egotism and arrogance. This shuts off inspiration from the actor's *Seele*. In order to have ideas, inspiration, talent, we must carry in our *Seele* the natural and self-evident feeling that there is an objective world that really can give actors something, and that it comes in to us: 'in-spiration' in the truest sense of the word.

Upon perceiving a world made up of a kingdom of artistic images, sounds, rhythms etc., the actor's *Seele* opens up, as if by itself, and frees up the path for each idea. This trust in the world of the imagination must be developed by actors as a fundamental awareness on the path to becoming more familiar with this world. Here we can enhance our diagram by drawing the world of artistic imagination as an indistinguishable (for now) cloud of fog. In the diagram it is drawn high up as something purely *seelisch-geistig*, in contrast to all that is physical, earthbound, heavy and material. In actual fact, this world of *Gestalten*, of the artistic imagination, is both within our *Seele* and all around us. (Figure II)

As we have said, the *Gestalten* of the imagination are moving, flowing, delicate entities. It is often hard to observe them and hold them in our consciousness. Much that arises in the imagination, especially in the early investigations of our work, may easily be lost. Just like a living being, an imaginary *Gestalt* has not only an outer but also an inner side, a body and *Seele*, and we must learn to 'observe' both. We will be able to perceive the *Gestalt*'s experiences, its inner *seelisch* traits, as soon as we awaken in ourselves empathy for the *Gestalt*, which will in turn be awoken in our *Seele* as we immerse ourselves in the imaginary *Gestalt*'s

Seele through the practice of attention and concentration as described previously.

Together, the *Gestalt*'s body and *Seele* form an organic, living whole. Everything in the *Gestalt* that is outwardly visible is a consolidation of the inner, the *seelisch*. The outer part of the *Gestalt*, its body, is far more delicate and transparent than with people in life. It is much more expressive, and that is self-evident because an <u>artistically</u>-observed imaginary *Gestalt* is an Idea-carrying, <u>synthesized</u>, *Gestalt* <u>type</u>. It is therefore the case that as artists, actors must have an inner ground from which to observe the imaginary *Gestalt*. This inner ground is always an artistic Idea. The actor may even be unaware of this Idea as it begins to work from the depths of the actor's *Seele*, invoking an imaginary *Gestalt* in the mind's eye. This inner ground is always available, and the more we train our imaginations, the more the *Gestalten* will take on their persuasive power.

Being purely *geistig*, an artistic Idea will consolidate itself into an imaginary *Gestalt*, a <u>synthesis</u> that is <u>of a type</u>, rather that the memory of some impression from life, a remembered 'photo' of something <u>particular</u>. The synthesized *Gestalt* type, as observed and created by artists, by actors, makes it possible for us to attain the greatest and most refined inner and outer harmony. For to observe the *Gestalt* is to create this *Gestalt*, in the same instant. With practice, actors can acquire great skill in creating by observing.

The imaginary *Gestalten* are not only able to move, but possess a powerful <u>ability to transform</u>. *Gestalten* can transform in accordance with the actor's will and also <u>by themselves</u>. They transform by themselves as they strive, so to speak, for a path to their most expressive and economical form. Indeed, the greatest possibility for perfecting our *Gestalten* lies in precisely this trait of theirs. Great artists have always known and widely relied upon these laws of the world of the imagination, and that the transformation process necessary for the completion of a Work requires time. Goethe, for instance, commented on one of his works: 'I have carried about this subject for forty years, so it has had plenty of time to purify itself of everything extraneous.' (Eckermann. Conversations with Goethe. 10 November 1823).

It is most important that actors carry within their *Seele* a firm trust in the ability of these *Gestalten* to transform. This trust, which we duly acquire through experience and long practice, awakens in the actor's *Seele* the necessary patience, and this plays a vital role in every artist's creative work. The *Gestalten* of the imagination possess another curious ability: they merge in the most remarkable way. When the need arises for two imagined *Gestalten* to do this, it occurs absolutely organically and there can be no question of a mechanical combination or fusion. Two *Gestalten* merge to become a third, new *Gestalt*. Although this newborn *Gestalt* possesses the traits of their forebears, it is nevertheless a completely independent *Gestalt* with its very own traits that only it can bring into the world of the imagination. But to create two *Gestalten* that merge into a third usually takes time, and sometimes a long, long time.

Actors may have in their imaginations two, three (or more) *Gestalten* for a part, and not know which to choose. This is very common, and often actors force the *Gestalten* to merge, or try to combine them into one mechanically, or choose one *Gestalt* and ignore the others. Such things are always artistically false and go against the laws governing the world of *Gestalten*. When numerous *Gestalten* appear in an actor's imagination for their part, there is always a reason. Each *Gestalt* carries within it something the actor needs for the part. All that is required is to work with them in the right way by offering the possibility to merge – something the *Gestalten* themselves are capable of and indeed desire – by allowing the time they need in order to do so.

So actors must learn to wait. However, this does not mean we remain passive and inactive. We continue working with the *Gestalten* that need to merge, without forcing or interrupting the process arbitrarily. That would be of no use. Through experience and patient practice, actors can learn about these secrets of the world of *Gestalten*. By making ourselves at home in that world, we soon notice that we develop a particular inner skill and sense a clear difference between tasteless, random imaginary forms and those that are, so to speak, 'lawful' and 'logical'. The realm of the imagination will no longer seem a place where absolutely anything is possible, where no 'laws' or 'logic' govern, where there is no imaginary truth. No longer will the words 'imagination' and 'falsehood' be synonymous, as is so often claimed these days. An actor's sense of taste will clearly expose arbitrariness and falsehood, and the lawfulness and truth of the imagination will prevail.

Speech

The field of artistically-formed human speech is a vast and to a certain extent separate field, and from it the arts of recitation and speech eurythmy stem as independent art forms. The full doctrine of speech formation cannot be described here and we will have to content ourselves with just a few remarks on the word in the art of the theatre.

The function of the spoken word on stage has, in our times, been greatly reduced. Nowadays stage speech has just one function (just as in ordinary everyday life): to express human thought. People now talk about feelings, about will impulses, but the feelings and will impulses themselves are not in their words. All that remains is declamation. However, in reality each sound in all of speech represents an entire world of the experiences of human beings, while the mental meanings of words are empty, lifeless abstractions. Human speech came about through human experience and it conceals and preserves within it everything the human *Seele* holds in its inner kingdom. Artists who deal with the word in their professions are able to recognize and revive the treasures lying concealed within speech. This is the only way their speech will be put to full use and be truly artistic, and play a primary role rather than the secondary one of merely passing on abstract thoughts, as is the case nowadays.

Take the sound 'A' for example.[1] If we pronounce this sound for a time and try to listen carefully, we will notice emerging from the sound a clear tendency to open oneself out. Our speech organ (mouth and larynx) opens, as when for instance we meet someone we like, to whom we wish to open up our whole being, and we will often exclaim a fulsome 'A–a!'. Our arms also tend to open wide, we open our being to them, and whenever this occurs undisturbed by external upbringing and finds form, it is expressed through an 'A'-sound. Similarly, when we encounter something that causes amazement, we also let out an 'A'-sound, albeit of a different colour. Again, we open ourselves to that which causes wonder, amazement in us. And when we suddenly understand something, something we were initially unable to grasp, we let out a delighted 'Ah!'. We open ourselves to what has suddenly been understood.

---

[1] The English phoneme /a:/ – as in 'father'.

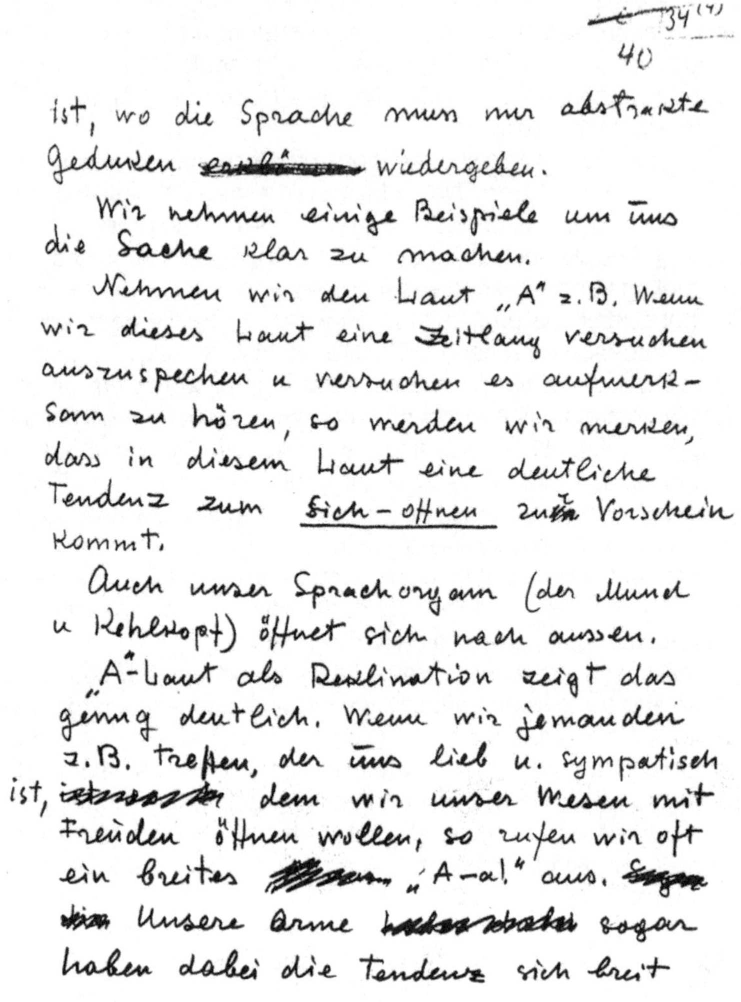

40

ist, wo die Sprache nun nur abstrakte
Gedanken ~~erklä~~ wiedergeben.

Wir nehmen einige Beispiele um uns
die Sache klar zu machen.

Nehmen wir den Laut „A" z.B. Wenn
wir dieses Laut eine ~~Zeitlang~~ versuchen
auszusprechen u. versuchen es aufmerk-
sam zu hören, so werden wir merken,
dass in diesem Laut eine deutliche
Tendenz zum Sich-öffnen zum Vorschein
kommt.

Auch unser Sprachorgan (der Mund
u. Kehlkopf) öffnet sich nach aussen.

„A"-Laut als Deklination zeigt das
genug deutlich. Wenn wir jemanden
z.B. treffen, der uns lieb u. sympatisch
ist, ~~etwas zu~~ dem wir unser Wesen mit
Freuden öffnen wollen, so rufen wir oft
ein breites ~~xxxx~~ „A-a!" aus. ~~Sogar~~
~~die~~ Unsere Arme ~~xxxxxxxx~~ sogar
haben dabei die Tendenz sich breit

FIGURE 18 *Page 40 of the 'Paris Manuscript'.*

As well as this 'opening-ourselves-up', we also find an 'A'-sound in order to 'lose ourselves', for instance when we come into pleasant company we may notice how we often involuntarily (meaning undisturbed by the intellect) let out a soft or perhaps even louder 'A–a'. We lose ourselves for a moment in the whole company. Or when we come in from the cold street into a warm room, and feel the need to, as it were, lose ourselves in this warmth, we also utter a soft and long 'A'. When we yawn, where our entire being wishes to lose itself in sleep, this too becomes an 'A'. A state of powerlessness often begins with the 'A-sound', and so forth. In this way we can detect the wisdom of human speech and the richness of sounds in the formation of words.

Let us take another sound as an example. Just as the 'A'-sound was formed by a *Seele* experience of opening-up, the 'U'-sound was formed by closing-in.[2] This is a sound that comes about when we experience fear, for instance, and all our inner forces gather and are pulled together. A strenuous, fearsome awakening expresses itself in the 'U'-sound. We must simply be able to differentiate the nuances.

Actors are able to discover the deeper, long-forgotten layers of *Seele*-meaning in words through sound, with endlessly richer means of expression than we are used to today. Artists of the word, actors can understand this by penetrating the secrets of words and sounds. Our feelings will grow and through such work we will go deeper, become stronger and more beautiful.

Let us take another example to see how wise and strong feelings are expressed in the formation of sounds. What happens in our *Seele* when something suddenly hurts? The first thing is a sharp need to see, to understand, to grasp <u>what</u> is it that hurts? All inner forces turn outwards ('A'). The second thing that happens, right away, is a drawing back of the *Seele* from the outer world, the pain, and also an anxious concentration on the feeling of pain ('U'). As this process proceeds rapidly the sound becomes an 'Au'. So when something suddenly hurts, it is 'Au!' that we cry out.[3]

---

[2] 'U' as in 'blue'.
[3] Generally written 'ow' in English.

We should briefly note that all sounds fall into two groups. We express <u>inner</u> states and experiences in vowels, while the consonants are felt in the <u>outer</u> events. Each word is a rich <u>picture</u> of that which occurs out in the world, and what humans themselves experience in their *Seele* through the outer. When compared to the rich image that a word's sound forms in the *Seele*, the mere <u>concept</u> of a word is quite dead and colourless. Only when actors penetrate such visual, meaningful word and sound feelings will their speech on stage become artistic. A good, great poet will always appear to readers as a painter and sculptor, whenever we sense the music of their sounds, rather than merely the content of the poem, which might also be understood in prose or some other form. The cold intellect of the present day cannot form any new words and no longer understands those created previously. But in the future, such creations will again be found and all artists whose creativity involves words should be encouraged to begin this great task.

Seelisch Atmosphere

We have spoken about artistic movement, imagination and speech. Now we must speak of another element that is strongly linked to how an artist works. Just as a living being needs to be surrounded by a sphere of air in order to exist, so too an artist's Work.

This atmosphere that actors need around them is of a purely *seelisch* nature: a *seelisch* atmosphere. Each and every human mood can also be described as a *seelisch* atmosphere, although we refer here not just to the little accidental moods often perceived on stage, but rather to the great power and significance of atmosphere in the art of theatre. It is not enough for an atmosphere on stage simply to emerge now and then as a faint mood, for it is too powerful a means of expression to be left without due attention on the part of the director and actors. Just as the speech, movements and situations of the play must be rehearsed, its atmospheres, with all their nuances and transitions, also need to be rehearsed. They must be properly found, properly distributed and performed. The atmosphere is the *Seele* of the performance. There can be no true art without atmosphere, without a *Seele*. And just as all artists, and actors as creative individuals, breathe this atmosphere, in and out, so too the audience, which is something of great significance for actors.

Technique without the *Seele* will always be a more or less completely soulless machine. This danger threatens the art of theatre, and rescuing the atmosphere for the art that is to come is one of the worthiest tasks of today's artists and actors. Without atmosphere the audience cannot become as one with the actors. They may perhaps think about this 'atmosphere-less' art, may understand it and marvel at the artist's technical dexterity, but they will never be able to feel as one with the actors in the higher magical realms of artistic consciousness, never be captured and persuaded by the actors' and director's art. And, more importantly, the audience will never help the actors to perform. Actors don't perform by themselves, independently – they perform with the audience's help. In every performance so much depends on the audience. All actors know this. Without atmosphere, all the positive forces that audiences are able to send actors during a performance (trust, sympathy, empathy etc.) will not be awoken in the audience and sent across onto the stage. However, when an audience experiences the same as the actors (or rather – as their *Gestalt*), then the artist's performance will be strengthened. This can only occur if actors radiate the necessary *seelisch* atmosphere, filling the entire theatre space with it and through it connect to the realm of the audience's artistic consciousness.

A great danger lies in creating a work of art without its corresponding atmosphere, something that occurs whenever an atmosphere remains only loosely formed. For instance, a pianist may play a musical piece and a certain atmosphere will be radiated. Another will produce quite a different atmosphere with the same piece, and with a third there will be no atmosphere present at all (although it may also be technically perfect). Actors who ignore the conscious task of maintaining and radiating the necessary atmosphere during a performance, will easily lose it among the many chance goings-on. They will, so to speak, be left without air, or submit themselves to an atmosphere that doesn't correspond to the moment. All this plays a decisive role in their creative work, and the director and actors' artistic ideas and goals can easily emerge as caricatures, or they may even evaporate altogether, simply because of a false atmosphere. Therefore actors must develop the ability, through the relevant exercises, to constantly maintain and radiate the necessary atmosphere.

An atmosphere can only exist on stage if the actors perform artistically and truthfully. Every artistic lie kills the atmosphere and a void emerges on stage. Actors must know that the greatest enemy of atmosphere is lying in art. Lying in life always creates an (evil) atmosphere. But on stage – never. Why? Someone who lies in life, in other words, who 'gives a good performance', their aim is always to conceal something, and as liars they create a certain atmosphere around themselves. On stage it is the other way around, the goal is always to reveal something, and actors who lie on stage, who perform badly, can reveal nothing, they create no atmosphere and cannot be taken seriously as a character.

It is only as a *Gestalt* that we can be taken seriously on stage, and a *Gestalt* cannot be present in a lie. In other words, the audience won't see a character or *Gestalt*, just an atmosphere-less nothing. On stage a lie can come about for two reasons. It is either an inner, *seelisch* lie, or it is an outer, physical one. It is *seelisch* when the actor doesn't know exactly what to perform, when the Idea for the part isn't clear or individual scenes aren't felt as part of the whole, but rather as independent episodes. A *seelisch* disharmony will then arise between the part and the play, and also between the actors. This disharmony is an artistic lie and it kills the atmosphere. A play that is well conceived and developed by the director is a guarantee against this sort of lie.

This inner disharmony also creates a physical lie. A badly conceived and developed part leads actors towards mistakes, which they sense during the performance, so they try to correct the inner disharmony through outer means. For instance, they strain the voice or their gestures wherever the *Seele* is too weak, or they start repeating words over again, in order to fill the *seelisch* void, or they make overly long pauses to show that something important is happening in the *Gestalt*'s *Seele*, whereas in reality they are again just masking an inner void, and so forth. This can also occur in cases where actors haven't found the inner structure of the part clearly enough and are misled by purely physical things. For instance, they may hold a pause longer than necessary merely because it makes them feel good and they're enjoying their state in this pause. Or they start enjoying their own voice, regardless of whether the moment is able to bear it. Either they laugh too much or cry too long, or perhaps they try to find a connection to the audience through pronounced physical means, and so on. All this only occurs if the part has no <u>inner content</u>, no *seelisch* skeleton, no guiding Idea that arranges all the play's scenes and details in order to harmoniously usher in a sense of the whole.

A purely physical lie on stage, meanwhile, arises through physical habits. An actor once produced a pleasing gesture, so it remains in their physical memory and they repeat this gesture without considering whether it suits <u>this</u> part. The gesture has long become meaningless and dead, nevertheless the habit causes the actor to find the dead gesture comfortable and so they apply it over again, creating a lie on stage that kills the atmosphere or prevents it from emerging in the first place. Many actors have a multitude of such dead habits, physical, vocal, and even of intonation.

Working correctly on the play, with the correct process for embodying the character and an acutely developed <u>feeling of truth</u>, frees actors from lies on stage. Actors must exercise to develop in their *Seele* and body a particular instinct for protecting and preserving themselves from all lies on stage, thereby clearing the path to the magical effects of atmosphere.

Rhythm

The same occurs with rhythm as with atmosphere. The higher artistic consciousness in its creative centre is itself a rhythmic being, and true creativity in artists can only proceed with rhythm. One can become familiar with the rhythm of life through certain exercises, and the rhythms that pulse all around are powerful means for stimulating and awakening artistic forces. All rhythmic exercises should aim to awaken a feeling for rhythm, to develop an organ, as it were, in the *Seele* of whoever is practicing. Such an organ will be able to perceive that which is rhythmical everywhere, in all forms, wherever it is manifest. And it is only when this organ begins to form that the theoretical can be properly understood and perceived.

If we consider everything that the director and actors have at their disposal on stage in order to artistically embody the author's Idea, we may say there is the action of the play, the scenery with its colours and forms, costumes, masks, *mise-en-scène*, movement, atmospheres, sentences, single words and sounds, feelings, the use of voice, *forte* and *piano*, tempo, pauses, metre etc. All these exist on stage in varying combinations, but a random, accidental combination of these elements is a rhythmic chaos, whose origins are found in everyday life, something cultivated by naturalistic theatre whenever it copies ordinary life.

Rhythmic lawfulness

Rhythmic lawfulness is the only force able to conquer chaos in art. But the lawfulness of rhythm is of a particular nature. It is not an outer lawfulness. It allows all possible combinations of the elements in its composition, renders an artist completely free, and in doing so it opens the doors to two opposing impulses: artistic freedom and inartistic randomness.

What is the difference between these two impulses? Artistic freedom flows from the artist's, the actor's higher consciousness. This is the direct effect of the artist's creative *geistig* centre. Inartistic randomness, on the other hand, is not linked to the artist's creative centre. It works from the lower levels of consciousness, which are all chaotic and which carry this chaos across into art. The artist's

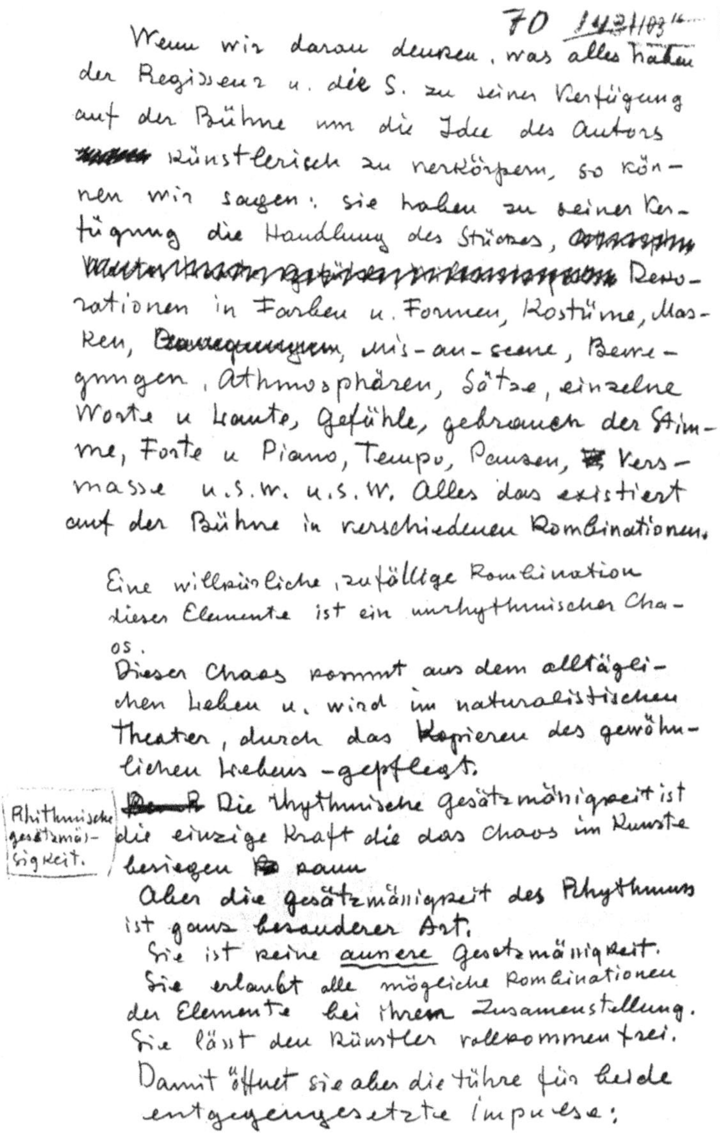

70 1421/03

Wenn wir daran denken, was alles haben der Regisseur u. die S. zu seiner Verfügung auf der Bühne um die Idee des Autors ~~waren~~ künstlerisch zu verkörpern, so können wir sagen: sie haben zu seiner Verfügung die Handlung des Stückes, ~~…~~ Dekorationen in Farben u. Formen, Kostüme, Masken, ~~Bewegungen~~, mis-en-scene, Bewegungen, Athmosphären, Sätze, einzelne Worte u Laute, Gefühle, Gebrauch der Stimme, Forte u Piano, Tempo, Pausen, Versmasse u.s.w. u.s.w. Alles das existiert auf der Bühne in verschiedenen Kombinationen.

Eine willkürliche, zufällige Kombination dieser Elemente ist ein unrhythmischer Chaos.

Dieser Chaos kommt aus dem alltäglichen Leben u. wird im naturalistischen Theater, durch das Kopieren des gewöhnlichen Lebens - gepflegt.

| Rhithmische gesetzmässigkeit. | ~~Da R~~ Die rhythmische gesetzmässigkeit ist die einzige Kraft die das Chaos im Kunste besiegen ~~ka~~ kann

Aber die gesetzmässigkeit des Rhythmus ist ganz besonderer Art.

Sie ist keine äussere gesetzmässigkeit.

Sie erlaubt alle mögliche Kombinationen der Elemente bei ihrem Zusammenstellung.

Sie lässt den Künstler vollkommen frei.

Damit öffnet sie aber die Türe für beide entgegengesetzte Impulse:

FIGURE 19 *Page 70 of the 'Paris Manuscript'.*

higher creative consciousness is aware of all the inner properties of the elements found in art. This is self-evident, because it is this very consciousness that animates and inspires artists and renders all such elements artistic. Only through the development of this consciousness will movement, words, the ability to imagine and qualities become artistic means of expression.

As with all forms and colours of the outer world, the features of this creative consciousness will be experienced inwardly. All this is quite impossible for the artist's lower consciousness. So randomness must prevail there.

Creative consciousness carries within itself inner lawfulness

Our higher creative consciousness carries within itself the inner lawfulness of artistic creation. This means: it carries within itself rhythmic impulses that truly merge all artistic elements.

Where should this inner lawfulness be sought?

Only in the realm of the artist's, the actor's higher consciousness.

How and in what form is this inner lawfulness rooted?

In no form. It has no need to be rooted, it is created anew each time. It doesn't repeat itself. It is absolutely free and flexible, for it is an <u>inner</u> lawfulness. One might say: there are as many <u>inner</u> artistic 'laws' as there are creative moments. That is artistic freedom.

Can these 'laws' be fully attained?

No. They spread out into the <u>eternity</u> of our ever-developing human consciousness. The path of the artist is always a <u>path</u>. For artists there is no <u>end of the line</u>. Such is the <u>greatness</u> of art.

What will show artists the <u>way</u> into this eternity? What are the signposts for artists wanting to evolve?

The inner 'laws' themselves. Although they stretch out into eternity, never becoming fixed anywhere and leaving actors completely free, they are nevertheless absolutely <u>CONCRETE</u> and are just as concrete at the outset as each inner step along the path into eternity.

There are three concrete inner 'laws' for merging all means of expression, and these correspond to three major forces that actors require in their profession:

<u>Truth</u> – transformed and elevated artistic thought
<u>Beauty</u> – the artist's purified feeling
<u>Goodness</u> – our will as heightened and strengthened through truth and beauty. Only a <u>strong</u> person, a <u>strong</u> artist can find goodness. All that is weak becomes a slave to evil.

This trinity is a signpost for artists and at the same time our ideal. Striving for this trinity is to make the <u>work of art rhythmic</u>, and the artist's higher consciousness lives in this trinity. The artist's creative consciousness is an entity that can never repeat anything. Everything that it creates is unique. So the way in which <u>this</u> artistic consciousness gives <u>that</u> Work rhythm (thereby making it true, beautiful and good) is individual and cannot be repeated. Every actor, every director must deepen the play's rhythms <u>afresh</u>, each time. We must have <u>complete trust</u> in our <u>artistic feeling</u>, or artistic intuition, which is the voice of the artist's creative consciousness, and it only emerges if a development process is present. Otherwise randomness looms with its destructive forces.

Once we not only understand but also <u>experience</u> this work, our impression will be that we're dealing with a <u>musical</u> piece, as if the musical and dramatic arts had become <u>organically synthesized</u>. And by bringing rhythm into our theatre, then actual sonatas and symphonies may come into being. Therein lies a great future for the theatre.

Artistic Individuality

We have spoken about the general acting technique and have described this as one of movement, imagination and speech. We have also spoken about atmosphere and rhythm, the mastery of which also belongs to our general acting technique.

Now we may ask ourselves: 'What sort of a force can this be, that is so powerful and through which our heavy body rises up, our imagination becomes invigorated, our speech refined and strengthened as a means of expression?' Our <u>seelisch-geistig</u> being is what must govern this force which invigorates us and lifts us up. Our higher consciousness, our artistic individuality, this is the force that is truly the artist within us. The artistic individuality inhales and exhales *seelisch* atmospheres, creating rhythms, it lives within them and is itself a rhythmic being. All physical, *seelisch* and *geistig* human traits, to the extent that they have become artistic, radiate from a centre, from the artist's creative individuality, and all exercises that actors practice should have only one aim: to release the forces of the artistic individuality, so that it may radiate through movement, imagination, speech, through atmospheres and rhythms.

But this is only one side of the matter. The other is that while working, we must always hold this thought clearly in our consciousness: 'I am practicing in order to free the path to my artistic individuality.' This thought, this feeling, this will, causes the forces of the individuality to be awakened and released, and then it will be possible for the individuality to help us in our work. In this way, we rise up towards our artistic individuality and the individuality descends to meet us.

It is possible to undertake certain *seelisch* and physical exercises without summoning the help of the artistic individuality, and these may achieve certain results. Great mobility of the body can be developed, but it will remain purely mechanical, and we can boost the activity of the imagination yet achieve nothing but memory-association abilities. We may also strengthen our speech organ so much that it becomes a mighty means of expression only able to express low feelings, emotions and instincts of the *Seele* and body. Even the powers of rhythm and atmosphere may be used but remain only at the service of our lower consciousness.

There is 'art' that is based on the lower strata of human nature, but it has no need for the powers of the awakened individuality. It is an opposite pole from art whose force of inspiration is the artist's individuality. It is important and decisive in every respect that actors <u>know</u> what these two types of art are like, and each must consciously follow our own artistic path. For if we do not and we follow it unconsciously, a great danger looms: even with the best will in the world we shall be tossed back and forth artlessly and passively on the waves driving human development.

Let us begin by considering art whose creative forces derive from human individuality, and recall our Figure II, where the actor's as yet undeveloped *seelisch*-physical traits were presented as a horizontal, earthbound line. The vertical line then showed these traits as having been developed and stimulated by the forces of the creative individuality.

Now we can extend our diagram: the artist's individuality, that of the actor, can be drawn here as a star that rises up <u>over</u> all physical and *seelisch* traits. It sends out its rays in two directions. Upwards – to the world of the creative imagination, and down – to our *seelisch*-physical traits, the actor's <u>means of expression</u>. We make them <u>transparent</u> both <u>to ourselves</u> and to our imaginary entities. (Figure III) This individuality is the being that alone chooses the *Gestalten* from the world of the imagination, transforms them and endows them with their own qualities, and it is in fact these qualities that make a work of art <u>individual</u>.

The higher the master's Work, the more the master's individuality shines out through that Work. And the power of the individual qualities, of the play, the part, is tremendous. For instance, it will depend entirely on such qualities whether King Lear is to be presented as a stupid old man, or as the tragic figure of a noble king, or as a great symbol of the worldly fate of life's impulses that have <u>grown old</u> yet remain majestic. It will depend on the qualities given by the individuality whether we judge or absolve

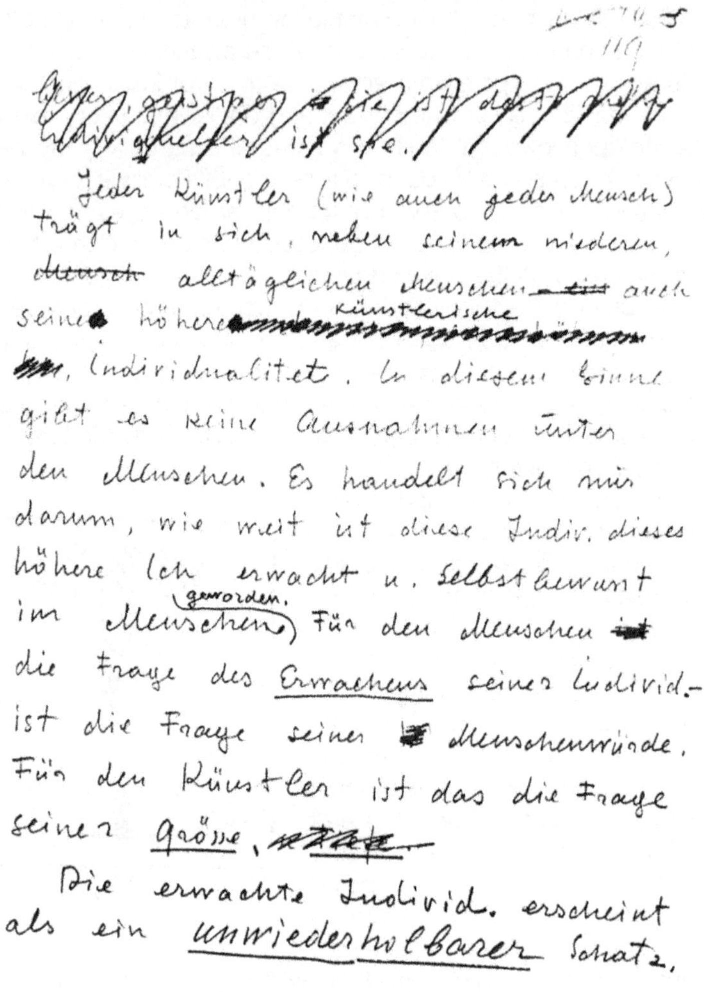

119

Jeder Künstler (wie auch jeder Mensch) trägt in sich, neben seinem niederen, ~~Mensch~~ alltäglichen Menschen ~~ist~~ auch seine höhere künstlerische Individualität. In diesem Sinne gibt es keine Ausnahmen unter den Menschen. Es handelt sich nur darum, wie weit ist diese Indiv. dieses höhere Ich erwacht u. Selbstbewusst im Menschen geworden. Für den Menschen ~~ist~~ die Frage des Erwachens seiner Individ.- ist die Frage seiner Menschenwürde. Für den Künstler ist das die Frage seiner Grösse.

Die erwachte Individ. erscheint als ein unwiederholbarer Schatz,

FIGURE 20 *Page 119 of the 'Paris Manuscript'.*

Shylock, whether Romeo has a pure, noble love *Geist*, or is just a hapless infatuated youth, whether Hamlet is a morbid visionary, or whether through his sufferings his *Geist* has penetrated the higher spheres of existence.

All artists carry within them both their lower everyday persona and their higher artistic individuality (as do all people). In this sense there are no exceptions among us, it is merely a question of the extent to which this higher self has become awakened and self-assured within us. For most people, the question of awakening their individuality is a matter of human dignity. For artists it is a question of their greatness. Once awakened, the individuality manifests itself as a treasure that can never be repeated. Individualities are never alike. The more self-assured an artist's individuality, the more they differ from all other artists throughout the ages.

True originality in an artist occurs through the awakening of their individuality. The less awake an artist's individuality, the more their lower nature takes the upper hand in their creative work, and the more they resemble many, many other artists. The artist's lower nature strives constantly to be original and singular and is forever condemned to remain the same as other lower natures. The more awake an artist's individuality, the broader their vision: they will constantly observe more and more of what is around them, will grasp (individually) all things until this perception of the world forms a *Weltanschauung*, and it is through this that an artist's individuality will be expressed.

Meanwhile, how does an artist's lower nature express itself? It expresses itself in opinions. Great individuals and artists in all eras have always striven for a single all-encompassing *Weltanschauung*, and hence have all been quite different. Conversely, the smaller, lower nature of individuals and artists always strives for different opinions, yet these always remain alike. Why is this so? Why does the opinion play such a minor role in the development of the human (artist's) vision, and why is the artist's individual *Weltanschauung* so decisive? Simply because this alone is able to embrace and inspire all three life forces of human beings: thinking, feeling, and willing. Conversely, an opinion will always remain superficial, without roots. And just as a consistent *Weltanschauung* harmonizes human thinking, feeling, and willing, a mere opinion will disrupt these three forces. (Or rather, a host of opinions: an opinion can never be alone since contrary opinions will always follow in droves).

Thinking, feeling, and willing, meanwhile, are the core forces that artists, actors need in their practice. These must be in good order, otherwise our practice may become disorderly, and this order can only form in an artist's *Seele* whose individuality is awakened through their *Weltanschauung*.

Weltanschauung

Artists make their *Weltanschauung* manifest through thinking, feeling, willing

We have already discussed how actors are artists who are both their own creation and the material at the same time. We create with our whole being, with our particular thinking, feeling, and willing, and by working from these main forces actors are able to reveal their reveal their *Weltanschauung* to audiences. The actor's practice is such that through each individual part that we play, we speak to the audience with our whole being. When an actor's creative self is harmonized through their individual *Weltanschauung*, this harmony affects the audience, and vice versa.

What is it that we value in the works of Raphael, Michelangelo, or Leonardo da Vinci? It is these artists' individuality. Why do reproductions and copies not satisfy us? Because their individuality cannot be reproduced and copied. That is the great mystery of the individuality, the mystery of art. We might also say: what is it great artists paint, write, compose, play? Themselves, their individualities, each <u>*Weltanschauung*</u>. Raphael's colours are the colours of his *Seele*, the colours of Raphael's feelings, his will impulses. Beethoven's will, his thoughts and feelings about the world and about life can be <u>heard</u> in his works. These great artists give us not only their works, they bestow on us each precious *Weltanschauung*.

Through their works they lend us their <u>eyes</u>, the eyes through which they <u>observe</u> the <u>world</u>. They become great magicians for us as they seek to show us <u>what</u> they alone are able to observe, and they <u>affect</u> our thinking, feeling, and willing, ennobling, refining and strengthening these powers within us. Furthermore, they summon us to their *Weltanschauung*. This artistic way in which they <u>speak</u> to us. Truly <u>persuasive</u> art will only come about when it is built upon a <u>persuasive</u> *Weltanschauung*.

An artist's *Weltanschauung* cannot be concealed

Perhaps we might wonder: 'There are surely artists who have not formed a *Weltanschauung*, therefore none can be expressed in their works.' The following can be said about this: every artist (just like any person), even if they haven't formed one consciously, have nevertheless a subconscious *Weltanschauung*, or at least a subconscious everyday relationship to the world. This relationship expresses itself with full force in each instant of everyday life. It expresses itself in everyday thinking, feeling, and willing. This still chaotic relationship to the world may remain completely subconscious, nevertheless it is present and has a constant effect on the outer world.

We can observe someone in everyday life and create a hypothetical *Weltanschauung* for them. Based on their actions, words, intonation, movements, wishes, feelings etc. we might ask: 'What would their *Weltanschauung* look like, if they had consciously got hold of it?' Occasionally it may even be a terrifying one, when consciously formulated, but that is not the important thing for the moment. What is important, rather, is that we cannot say some artists have no *Weltanschauung* and therefore leave audiences unaffected by it. An effect will always radiate from the artist's whole presence, so it is just a question of whether the artist, the actor, works consciously, is accountable and controlled, or whether subconsciously, and is therefore unaccountable and uncontrolled.

An artist's *Weltanschauung* permeates their entire practice

Every artist evolves through their *Weltanschauung*, their *Weltempfindung*, or through their subconscious relationship to the world. Every artist has the need to give expression to their *Weltanschauung* or *Weltempfindung*, and this can occur in various ways, depending on the means of expression, on whether the artist paints, writes or acts this intuitive relationship to the world.

The *Weltanschauung* penetrates deeply into an artist's, an actor's inner life and actions. For instance, when two actors work on the same piece, the type of movement, speech, will be different in each actor, as will the entire nature of their respective imaginations. The less awake the actor's individuality, the less conscious their *Weltanschauung*. The more their means of expression will resemble the means of the expression of other actors who haven't yet penetrated some sort of conscious *Weltanschauung*. A template will emerge, always a sign that an actor hasn't yet developed anything entirely of their own to say through their art and share with the audience.

An actor's individuality and their *Weltanschauung*, their essence and entire activity always penetrate everything they do, powerfully, from the highest layers of their consciousness to the smallest physical movements.

Weltanschauung that has no effect on art

We have briefly characterized art whose creative power arises from the artist's individuality, and seen how an actor's work of art will be made original by an individual *Weltanschauung*. There is, however, an exception to this, a type of *Weltanschauung* that is neither linked to the creative forces of the individuality nor derived from the individuality or higher consciousness, but rather from small, isolated regions of the consciousness. This *Weltanschauung* is the product of abstract and merely mental thinking, in other words it is materialistic (with all its branches).

Any art bound up with such a *Weltanschauung* cannot build on the forces of the individuality, for every *Weltanschauung* is an eye through which the world is viewed, and we may ask: how do materialistic eyes view the world? What do these eyes observe in the world around them? They see matter. And they wish to see only matter. It is not our individuality that looks through such eyes, but the intellect. The objectivity of a materialistic *Weltanschauung* is a striving for a <u>uniform view</u> of everything, with nothing being particular, in other words no <u>individual</u> view, because this seeing is by its very nature common to all. We all see matter in the world and this requires neither a higher consciousness nor an awakened individuality. Similarly, materialism has no need to obscure its precise gaze with the forces of our higher consciousness. The impressions of the material world are thus combined through a complicated process of mental speculation, being thereby suspended in a materialistic *Weltanschauung*. Here the intellect is not placed at the service of our higher consciousness, rather it sees itself as the higher and ultimate being. Its speculative activity creates a border between our lower and higher consciousness.

For artists, for actors, it means that their individuality, the true 'artist' within, remains on this side of the border, inactive, unable to cross over. Materialism as a *Weltanschauung* does create its own art to suit itself. In this art all the lower forces of human nature, not having been purified by the individuality, are put to use and are guided by the intellect. What emerges is an intellectual art, art created by the intellect entirely in the realm of the natural world. A characteristic of this art is that it is completely bereft of imagination, since the realm of the imagination (with its individual forces) lies beyond the threshold that the intellect has built. Imaginary impressions cannot penetrate this threshold. Furthermore, the intellect is a powerful, cunning combiner. Through its clever and quick-witted combinations of objective facts found in nature, it substitutes the imagination.

Now, when we consider which specific means of expression naturalistic art has created, then we must say: none. Its means of expression all derive from nature. Everything is expressed just as it is expressed in natural life. 'Just like real life' – that is the highest ideal of naturalistic art. Here actors are not required to be an individuality, and nor do they need a *Weltanschauung*, not even a materialistic one (although naturalistic art itself obliges them to behave on stage as if they were supported by such a thing). All that naturalistic theatre demands of its actors is an impassioned nature and the ability to copy life.

Theatre Now and in the Future
The fate of noble works in naturalistic theatre

We may infer several consequences of the present-day naturalistic theatre, which presents plays that often touch on interesting ethical, philosophical or religious problems, but seeks through its means of expression to make the author's Work look exactly as if such things had taken place in real life. The problem explored by the author is present, the audience understands it, can discuss it, and so on, but the question arises: what has the theatre itself brought to the issue? Why couldn't it <u>simply</u> have been left in a book, or made intelligible to the audience in a lecture? Nothing could be simpler. When a play is given by performers embellishing it with natural passions and feelings that are familiar to us all, it falls short of creating a work of stage art based on the author's Work, which is inevitably left flattened, mundanely coloured, and loses its propensity for noble refinement and idealistic greatness.

Often naturalistic actors aren't even aware that certain parallel *Seele* states border each other so closely that they can easily be confused, but which are in fact quite different. Each pair of states is made up of a noble part leaning towards the individuality, on the one hand, and on the other an everyday element leaning towards nature. Some examples:

> Anger – Malice
> Love – Passion
> Fear – Anxiety
> Kindness – Politeness
> Purpose – Effort

And so on. Through the embellishment of passion and feelings whenever performers play naturalistically, the audience is <u>forced</u> to receive and consider the conflict presented by the author (however noble it may be) merely with their everyday psychology.

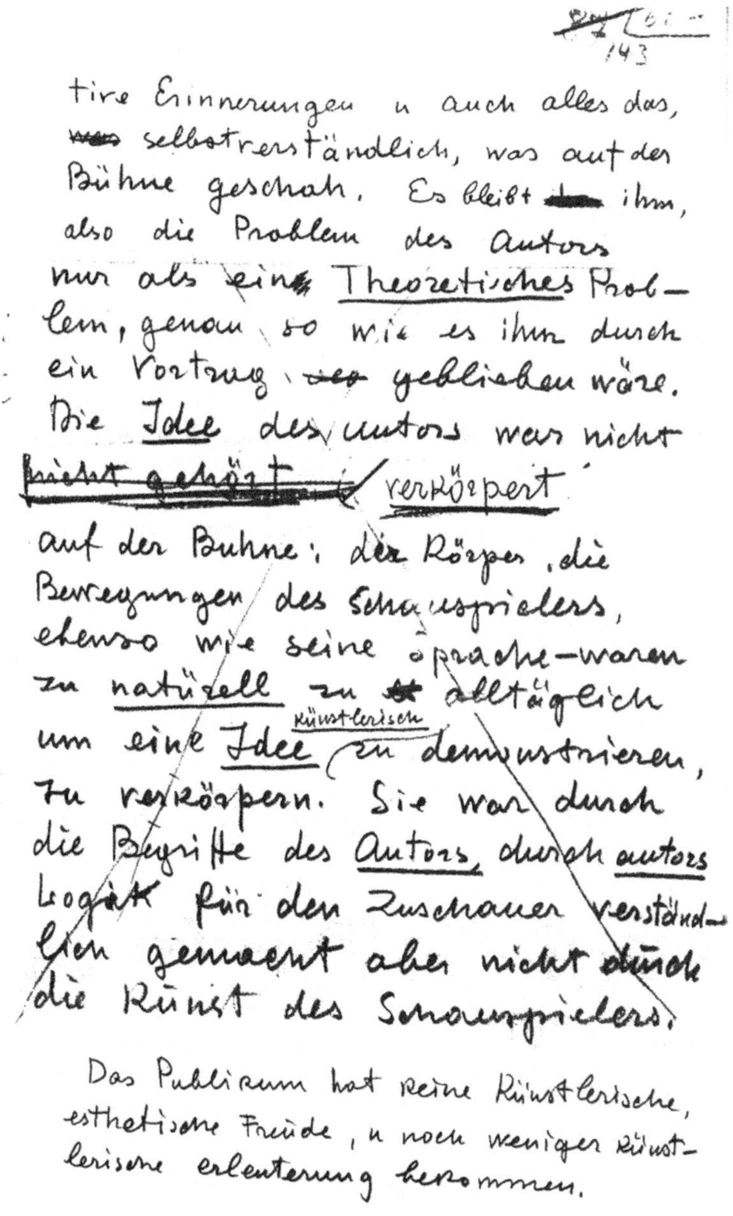

143

tire Erinnerungen u auch alles das, ~~was~~ selbstverständlich, was auf der Bühne geschah. Es bleibt ~~ihm~~ ihm, also die Problem des Autors nur als ~~eine~~ Theoretisches Problem, genau so wie es ihm durch ein Vortrag ~~des~~ geblieben wäre. Die Idee des Autors war nicht ~~nicht gehört~~ verkörpert auf der Bühne; der Körper, die Bewegungen des Schauspielers, ebenso wie seine Sprache – waren zu natürell zu ~~ae~~ alltäglich um eine ~~Idee~~ künstlerisch zu demonstrieren, zu verkörpern. Sie war durch die Begriffe des Autors, durch autors Logik für den Zuschauer verständlich gemacht aber nicht ~~durch~~ die Kunst des Schauspielers.

Das Publikum hat keine künstlerische, esthetische Freude, u noch weniger künstlerische erleuterung bekommen.

FIGURE 21 *Page 143 of the 'Paris Manuscript'.*

The audience's fate

What happens to the audience when they watch a noble theme performed through naturalistic means of expression? The author's noble Idea will be clothed in everyday, ordinary psychology, so this resonates in the everyday psychology of the audience. The audience experience <u>their own</u> psychology being awakened through the everyday psychology on stage. They receive nothing new, nothing that rises <u>above</u> their everyday psychology. They aren't elevated and <u>woken up</u> to <u>new</u> experiences, so they go deeper into <u>themselves</u>, into their own affective memories, which correspond to the feelings being shown on stage. They settle into a doze, so to speak, slumbering in their own affective memories. This can be very satisfying, but anyone who daydreams does just this, and in principle the art of the theatre is not needed for this activity. During a naturalistic performance the audience remain <u>in themselves</u>. They are only outwardly <u>in the theatre</u>, inwardly however they are 'at home'.

And just as our affective memories are often quickly forgotten, once the impulses are no longer present, so too with the audience, who forget the affective memories experienced 'in the theatre', along with everything, of course, that took place on stage. The author's problem remains a <u>theoretical one</u>, just as it would have been in a lecture. The author's Idea wasn't <u>embodied</u> on stage, the actors' bodies, movement and speech were too <u>natural</u>, too everyday to artistically demonstrate and embody an <u>Idea</u>. It was made comprehensible to the audience through the <u>author's</u> definitions, through the <u>author's</u> logic, rather than through the actor's art. The audience will have received no artistic, aesthetic joy, let alone artistic enlightenment, and the result of such attempts at embodying noble ideas or feelings through naturalistic theatre is always disharmony. Naturalism has made its judgement: 'It is no longer a time for obsolete idealistic themes,' while failing to recognize that its own art, being built on a materialistic *Weltanschauung*, can have no organic effect on noble ideas, themes and feelings.

Naturalism is a transitional form of stage art

Nevertheless, such efforts are meaningful and symptomatic for all those seeking new paths in art in the theatre. What is the significance of such efforts? When a noble Idea, on the one hand, and a naturalistic means of expression on the other, come into contact, a struggle arises between them. The Idea wishes to lift, so to speak, the naturalistic means of expression to a higher sphere. The naturalistic means of expression, on the other hand, wants to flatten the Idea and allow it to sink to a lower sphere. Neither prevails definitively, so both remain in a disharmonic sphere. How can one understand this point? It means that naturalism is not a definitive and self-contained form of art. If it were, a noble Idea wouldn't have any place at all in naturalistic theatre. Or naturalistic theatre wouldn't know where to begin with such Ideas. Today's naturalistic theatre is a turning point, a battleground on which the possibilities for the future are contested. We must know this in order to be able to consciously take part.

Another question arises: which possibilities for the future does today's naturalism in the theatre contain? We shall find answers to this question when we recall that theatre originated in the ancient mysteries, in other words from a consciousness in which our three main forces of thinking, feeling and willing, were held as a harmonious whole, before the days when science opposed religion, before there was any art that wanted nothing to do with wisdom, and an all-encompassing *geistig* Weltanschauung prevailed. This is the past of our theatre.

Theatre today

As the intellect began to develop within us, a great need to feel independent gradually arose, to become free from the all-encompassing *Geist*. The intellect, which strives for concreteness and analysis, began to see and examine everything around us separately, so the limitless *Geist* was abandoned, forgotten by us for a time. We took a step down. We became interested in our own *Seele*, rather than the all-embracing *Geist*. And just as today's analytical science emerged, so too did our present-day art that concretely observes and copies life. Under centuries of pressure from the intellect, art descended from the *Geist* to the *Seele* and eventually concentrated its whole interest on the *Seele*, thereby becoming psy<u>cho</u>logical. And the intellect also plays a major psy<u>cho</u><u>log</u>ical role. This is where the theatre is today.

However, features of the future theatre are also present. On the battleground of naturalism we can already clearly see the signs of two directions for the future, one leaning towards matter, the other towards the *Geist*. Naturalism can (and will) split into two contrary directions, and it will eventually disappear, for it is just a transition stage in the art of theatre.

Mechanistic art

The first direction will emerge under the influence of the intellect as it develops further and strives for what is most concrete to our outer senses: matter. It will increasingly comprehend and master matter and its laws, and the more these are mastered and conquered through the power of the intellect, the more it will find movement, in complicated ways and through complex laws. It will intrude more and more on people's lives, and the more people become dependent on the now-moving matter, the more life will start to resemble a mechanism. The moving matter, the mechanism, will work like a spell on people, and this spellbinding power will develop because the more complete the mechanism, the more it will resemble the human intellect. A powerful intellect that has become mechanistic in the service of human beings will influence humans like a magic spell.

This sense of awe of the mechanistic will cost humankind dearly. Through naturalism, which is so strongly linked to everyday life and which copies life with complete accuracy, this mechanism is carried over onto the stage. And it is here, in the realm of art, that artists who choose the mechanistic path will have to pay the mechanism with their own *Seele*. The mechanism of the future will be able to completely supplant a *Seele* weakened by the absence of the *Geist*. Even now, where this mechanism in the arts is still only on a baby step, we can already see, here and there, how humans are being supplanted by the machine. Actors' movements, their gait on stage, are being replaced by skipping and sliding across constructions, going on moving walkways etc. Because of the mechanism, actors' movements, so expressive when they are *Seele-* and *Geist*-filled, are becoming drained of both.

Attempts have already been made to express the state of an actor's state of mind through a moving wheel, instead of their performance, with changing colours and sounds whenever there was a change in the character's state of mind. We have long grown accustomed to such theatrics, and in doing so we disown the beauty and expressive possibilities of the human body. Instead of developing the actor's body and penetrating the *Seele* from within, we give it the static form of a mask, killing it, leaving it unused, undeveloped, existing for nothing. The artist's imagination will also become lifeless and its entire strength turn outwards: the set and stage space in general will cause the entire attention of the artist working mechanistically to be directed outwardly. Instead of using the imagination for inner work, the artist's energy is turned outwards through mass, number and weight. The changeability of the stage space is no longer understood inwardly, enabling people to alter the inner meaning of the space by their presence, but rather the stage space becomes purely mechanistic and needs to be presented to the audience via tremendous, complicated processes.

The artist's word is replaced in part by mechanistic expressive sounds and noises, while the word itself is used merely for explaining the mental sense. It is no longer be important <u>how</u> the word is spoken, whether it was chosen or crafted for the audience. The entire weight of the word is transferred to the <u>what</u>, to the logical and intellectual. New words are formed, yet their source is not the inner life, instead they pursue the convenience of mental understanding.

Art of the free individuality

The other direction is one whose first signs and first steps this present book as a whole seeks to characterise. It stands in opposition to the mechanistic one described above, since its intent is to preserve the artist's *Seele*, as well as attempting to take the additional step of stimulating the artist's *Geist* and their individuality.

However, this striving for the *Geist* is not a return to the general *Geist* of the past. That would be impossible, because the awakened and developed intellect will now also have its own claims on any art striving for our *Geist*. The *Geist* that the new art strives for is a concrete, no longer all-embracing *Geist*. It will be sought quite concretely by artists everywhere and in every manner, and presented in an artistic form. Above all, though, it will be concretely observed in the artists themselves. All creative methods presented here are like a wake-up call for the artistic individuality. The entire ethos of the theatre work being cultivated here is a path to the actor's individuality. The first steps in awakening the individuality are what is important. The actor's individuality will gradually come across certain artistic problems by itself and seek to solve them.

The development and unfolding of the individuality is an unlimited process and over time it can develop great artistic powers. Just like a focal point, the artist's individuality will amass all that is *geistig* into our art. The newly-grasped and trained language will reveal to actors the manifold but concrete wealth of everything that is *geistig*-creative, a new type of movement that gives us the gift of the countless possibilities of artistic expression. This will lift us high over the naturalistic, limited realm of movement and our imaginations will with practice awaken an exactness that reveals the *Gestalten* of the imagination in a truly concrete way. Actors sometimes feel they suffer from a certain poverty of the imagination, but it is often not poverty at all, but rather the imagination's imprecision. As long as their imagination remains imprecise and without sufficient training, they are forced to make do with the everyday naturalistic imaginary forms. With the correct development of the imagination, though, actors will be able to see a whole new horizon.

As Goethe himself wrote: 'Someone who has been born into and trained in the so-called exact sciences, at the height of their powers of reason, will not easily comprehend that there is also an exact sensorial imagination, without which art is essentially inconceivable.' Actors will uncover a new feeling for characters and for their inner path, a new artistic concreteness for the composition of their parts. The method for seeking the play's Idea, the score of atmospheres for the performance, the method of 'putting questions' to the world of *Gestalten*, all such things will place the entire *geistig* concreteness of our art within our reach.

This fully conscious activity differentiates the new actor (and artists in general) from earlier ones, where everything was built only and exclusively on artistic intuition. Artists and actors of today, and particularly of tomorrow, can no longer build their practice on the forces of the intuition alone. Humankind's intellectual development has already grown so great and powerful, and the new actor must not lose sight of this.

The intellect must be used by the artist to grasp and become familiar with their trade, both from an ethical-ideological point of view and through the technical engagement in their daily work. The actor's intellect must not create, it must only bring knowledge, and in this way the artistic intuition will always remain fresh and active. Conversely, if the intellectual powers are discarded and we try to rely on artistic intuition alone, actors will sink into a general, vague *geistig* condition, an old, bygone *geistig* world.

In other words, a positive side of naturalism must be recognized and carried forward, a familiarity with and love of that which is concrete. All that is dreamlike that flows into the void has been forever conquered by naturalism. And that is what naturalism has bequeathed the future. The future will be grateful for this clear vision that naturalism has trained in us. Thus both tendencies of the theatre of the future emanate from naturalism and may step into the future in its place. In order to consciously follow these paths, actors of today must make a choice to the seek the paths of individual art, and then the means of expression of the performing arts must be transformed. All well-meaning wishes for the renewal of the theatre will be futile if actors do not renew themselves. The actor is the lead part in theatre and we alone can bring life to these new paths and make them concrete.

All that we have been discussing may be summarized in the following diagram.

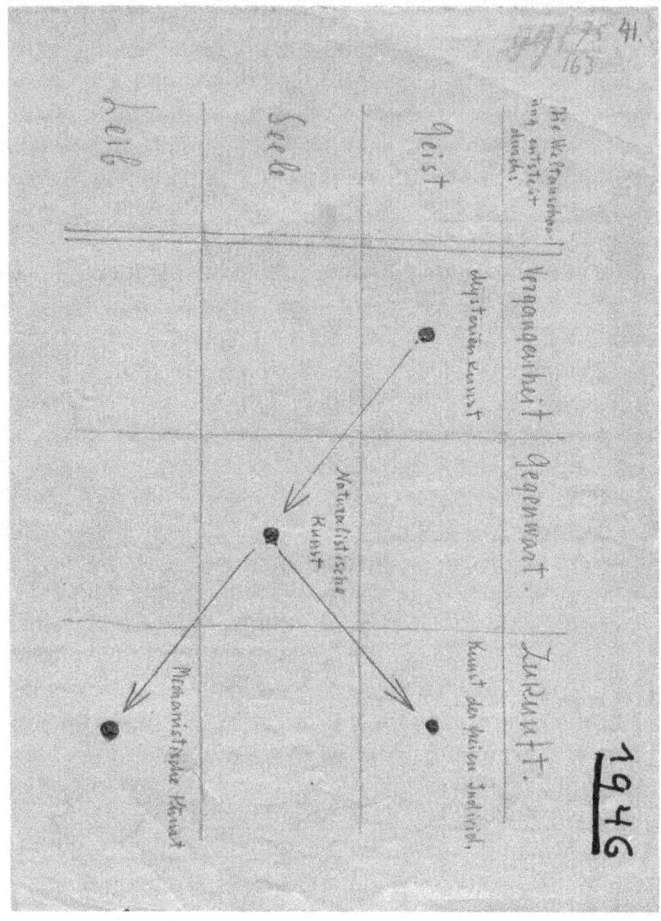

FIGURE 22 *Original diagram on page 163 of the 'Paris Manuscript'.*

Translation:

Weltanschauung comes about through:	Past	Present	Future
Geist	Mystery art		Art of the free individuality
Seele		Naturalistic art	
Body			Mechanistic art

Character and Destiny
Weltanschauung as a technical-professional matter

We now return to the importance of our *Weltanschauung*. Nowadays, this issue and the question of whether a *Weltanschauung* exists within us is seen as a private, even intimate matter. But a time will come when this will be different, when artists understand enough about the powerful and decisive role the *Weltanschauung* plays in all human work of a *geistig* nature, when this matter will be considered a technical-professional one. For anyone involved in *geistig* work, the *Weltanschauung* is their *geistig* toolkit. And this simple truth will be understood and recognized. As *geistig*-workers, actors have a very particular profession. The result of our *geistig* work is such that when it is taken seriously, it leads to a fully responsible artistic conscience, with our creative *Geist* supplying, for instance, the character and character destiny. How could one responsibly achieve such results without a *Weltanschauung*? We develop our general education at school and acquire specialist training at university, but these are national, state affairs, not personal, intimate. Our *Weltanschauung* can and must be formed in the same way and this is precisely how actors should approach it.

How can the first steps be taken, the initial impulse to consciously begin developing our *Weltanschauung*? Well, the actor's field of expertise is human character, its inner path and progress along it, leading up towards the light, to brightness, or down into the darkness: the inner and outer destiny. So we must begin with human character. Just as scholars read their specialist literature, actors must do the same in their field. They should systematically study the biographies of notable people, and in doing so create a living image of the character in their imagination. They must become well acquainted through both their biographies and their works, and by doing so actors will acquire a new feeling for what a human being truly is. A new sense of character will gradually develop and grow and lead to significant results not only in our artistic work, but in everyday life too.

In working with biographies, actors must also try to clearly picture the inner <u>path</u>, the inner journey of the character described in the biography, and to follow them with compassion. How did the character being described develop inwardly? Which thoughts, feelings, interests, desires did they have when younger, and how did these develop later? What external or inner factors affected this transformation? What remained unaffected? We must create a clear, vivid and truthful living image of the character's transformation and strive to ultimately understand why and how they became different in old age from their youth. Actors must organize their study of biographies in such a way that they understand not only the character's inner (and hence outer) path, but also the <u>direction</u> their whole life took. Across their life, their thinking, feeling and willing, what they created, through luck and misfortune, the character sways constantly between good and evil. The character may themselves remain unaware or partially aware of this, but for actors working with their biographies everything must be clear and we must strive for a true understanding of what life made of this particular character. Did it lift them up inwardly and improve them, making them self-confident, free, good, and strong, or did it crush, weaken them, making them wicked, anxious, and so forth?

Actors will gradually get a sense of character not only of people we have personally known for a long time. We all observe and get a sense of those we know well, love or hate, much more than people we meet by chance. Now, once our capacity for observation has grown and increased, we will already after the briefest of conversations perceive a human character. This is of great significance for actors, to achieve a deeper vision of characters while at the same time forming greater awareness in the creation of our *Weltanschauung*. Such work develops in actors a sensitivity, awakens in us an artistic intuition for understanding and deepening our parts. The characters we portray will no longer be dead outlines. No longer will they be like many movie heroes, for instance, reacting to random outer events – they will enjoy an inner world and be guided by it. Such actors will allow audiences to sense <u>life</u> during the performance, an inner drama, not just outer randomness. Only an inner path can justify before an audience the play's and character's outer events on stage, and this is a further brick for building up our *Weltanschauung*. We will acquire a greater feeling for the meaning of life and be able to portray our parts as complete, significant human lives, as inner characters in an outwardly harmonious form.

Character = path = meaning = feeling, these will form a whole. This whole is: <u>a sense of destiny</u>.

Destiny will gradually emerge as a <u>wise guide</u>, and without this wisdom of character destiny we cannot get a proper sense of what <u>destiny</u> means.

Sociocultural character

The next thing actors can do to further enrich and refine their artistic capabilities and develop a *Weltanschauung* – once again, as specialist technical work – is to become acquainted with the psychology of different sociocultural groups. Every group has its own task in the world, its voice in the history of humankind and its own goal. Actors should penetrate the *Seele* of different sociocultural groups, in a purely artistic manner and with no need to carry out any research scientifically, but by simply beginning to notice everything that we already carry in our *Seele* through ordinary observations about the life of that group. All that is recalled should immediately be turned into an image, rather than left as a series of abstract thoughts. Everything must be transformed by our artistic imagination into a *Gestalt*, so that all that is detected about this social group, whether from a newspaper or a great work of art, or a notable personality that suddenly arrives on the scene in that sociocultural world – all impressions received are artistically transformed to form an image of the group's character.

A traditional, well-known work of art belonging to a sociocultural group will reveal to the working actor deep and meaningful secrets about the group's *Seele*. It is just a question of the inner activity with which we engage our artistic attention in seeking and transforming the material. Folk myths, sagas and legends provide great, valuable material for developing a sociocultural group's imaginary *Gestalt*.

Sociocultural group destiny

We should also penetrate a sense of a whole sociocultural group's destiny, just as we did for individuals. We would do well to study history, but again, only in a purely artistic way, not by learning historical facts by heart, but rather by transforming history into artistic images. We must follow the inner (and outer) path of the group's destiny, just as we did with individuals, and penetrate their wise ways. Through this work, actors will gradually be able to hear, so to speak, a sociocultural group's voice, and become ever more alert and penetrate deeper into the group's imaginary *Gestalt*, as if with new eyes and ears, further strengthening the actor's *Weltanschauung*.

Actors who hold such a kingdom in their *Seele*, a sense of a sociocultural group and its destiny and its artistically imagined *Gestalt*, will acquire a great artistic power for prophecy. We will no longer be capable of portraying someone in our own or from an unfamiliar sociocultural group in a superficial or senseless manner. Through the *Gestalt* of each part played, we will be able to offer audiences a great artistically-created truth. It will no longer satisfy our artistic intuition to portray a national type that needs nothing but a costume, mask, or perhaps an accent, in order to be recognized. The actor's artistic intuition will let the voice of that sociocultural group ring out through each part. This will occur in a highly refined manner, like harmonics in music, like a vocal timbre. However, we mustn't think such work can ever be brought to an end, that one day a conclusive sociocultural group *Gestalt* will be found and formed. This is neither possible nor necessary; the work must be simply begun and carried out, and the rest may be left to time.

Through such intense work, actors will experience the loveliest, finest aspects of our art. We will increasingly wean ourselves off the idea that we are audience-entertainers, and it will gradually come about that actors recognize our profession as an important cultural factor. All such work brings many unexpected positive results, for instance it mitigates the present-day blindness of the *Seele*, the result of this great hatred of peoples that wraps itself around the Earth, this political hysteria is poison for those who feel the need to penetrate an awareness of people. This hatred will rule over humankind for a long time and we cannot wait until order is restored. We must work patiently as artists in order to isolate ourselves from this hatred.

Gestalt

All the work described above forms elements for creating a *Gestalt* of the ideal character. This noble *Gestalt*, which actors carry as artists in their imaginations, forms an inexhaustible source of energy for their creative work. This imaginary *Gestalt* will contain powerful feelings and will impulses, as if condensed, and through it an actor will acquire a concrete sense of the greatness of the *Seele*. All parts played by the actor will seem different. It is very common for some artists, actors, throughout life and in their professional work, to gradually form habits of certain *seelisch* qualities. These habits render actors blind as artists. Through such habits the distance that keeps our vision fresh is lost, and they no longer see objectively what they are playing. It no longer excites them as artists, as if everything were familiar and they'd already played everything possible, and their work no longer brings any pleasure. This is artistic blindness.

Actors who gradually develop the *Gestalt* of the ideal character in their imaginations will find that it will constantly elucidate and illuminate every part like a powerful ray of light. The great distance that forms between the part and the ideal *Gestalt*, this is the distance that allows actors to observe their part with complete objectivity and constantly measure the character's *Seele* using a fresh set of scales. By the light of the imagined ideal *Gestalt*, actors are able to observe the smallest aspect of our part just as easily as the greatest. And these small details – that may previously have gone quite unnoticed, having neither the distance nor a ray of light from the imagined *Gestalt* – now appear as marks of a great and vital apparition, and their acting acquires a special brilliance. This brilliance can be seen in many different details, all deriving and speaking from a single origin of meaning. The *Gestalt* of the ideal character will give us this inner virtuosity, an elevated mastery to observe and portray.

In the world of the imagination, actors do not 'see' as in life with our ordinary eyes. We 'see' our *Gestalt*, so to speak, <u>from all sides at the same time</u>. We must examine the entire form and plastic shape, all colours of the outer *Gestalt*, as if we were all at once at all points in the space. We also 'see' our *Gestalt*'s *Seele*. In the same <u>instant</u>, we examine the whole wealth of experiences that belong to the character and that will only be able to be developed before an audience over time. It is as if one could suddenly grasp another person's entire destiny, their whole life from birth to death. How amazing they would appear to us! It is precisely so with actors and their characters. This work of observing in the world of *Gestalten* with an altered sense of space and time affects actors in a particular way: it gradually imbues them with the character's force and the ability, so to speak, to radiate something whole, irrespective of any theatrical resources. Even during the performer's first entrance on stage the audience must sense, through this radiating, something of the destiny of the entire part. It is not just through the make-up, costume, movement, type of speech etc. that the destiny of the character is to be understood, it must also be felt through this radiating. If actors are able to sense their parts like this, then so will the audience, and regardless of which words are spoken, which actions performed, whether the part is large or small, audiences will sense and experience a character type with its destiny and atmosphere. Such is the actor's lofty task.

Parallel to the formation of the *Gestalt* for the ideal character and this noble wisdom, actors must form an imaginary *Gestalt* for evil. We must acquire a more refined sense of evil, so that our artistic portrayals of evil aren't overly primitive. Every theatrical play that is truly a work of art will always present a battle between good and evil in one form or another. Without a particular and refined view of these two forces, actors will, in our portrayals of characters, be forced to shape them within the confines of primitive forms. Furthermore, we must learn to discern between two main forms of evil, both its ugly and beautiful, seductive forms. Actors will never be short of material for forming the *Gestalt* through these two forms of evil, whether in life, in art, fairy tales and sagas etc. Our art will acquire a certain two-layered nature lifting all that we create to a higher level, and we will no longer play evil as evil and good as good, for such things will seem too primitive and tasteless. We will know the original sources as being good and evil, but the masks that veil the appearance of good and evil will become complex and artistic. As Stanislavski used to say: 'When you play a good person, first find where they are bad.' The concept of the part and the play will become inexpressibly more refined in actors working in this way. Not only will we understand the literal sense of their part, but intuitively discern the original source from which the words flow.

We recognize a painter's simple portrait as a worthy work of art, if through the image the artist reveals something about the character that they themselves hadn't known before. Something that affords them self-knowledge. And it is always something related to good or evil. One of art's most important tasks is: to show that which is not immediately apparent, and artists can only do this if they have trained their intuition to sense the two-layered nature of such manifestations. What is the artist's *Weltanschauung* in this analysis? It is the vision of such a world-mask belonging to whoever the artist is, that has never been envisioned before. And what is such an artist's creative work? It is to show the eternal forces of good and evil through these masks that the artist envisions in their particular way, and has made transparent. No one need reinvent good and evil, and artists needn't concern themselves with these forces, but rather with the masks of these forces. The more elementary and primitive the manner in which actors show good and evil on stage, the less significant will be their Works. Or, conversely: the less an actor is able to grasp good and evil as it is, without a veil, the more elementary, primitive and less significant will be the masks with which they endeavour to work on stage.

In this way actors may forge further along the path towards a *Weltanschauung*, while giving our individuality the *seelisch-geistig* sustenance that it requires. Character, character destiny, a sense of the inner path and the meaning of the character's life, a sense of a sociocultural group's *Seele* and imaginary *Gestalten* for the ideal character and for evil forces – these all nourish an actor's individuality, as well as refining the actor's artistic practice to such an extent that we come ever closer to the forces of our individuality. This is the meaning of such work.

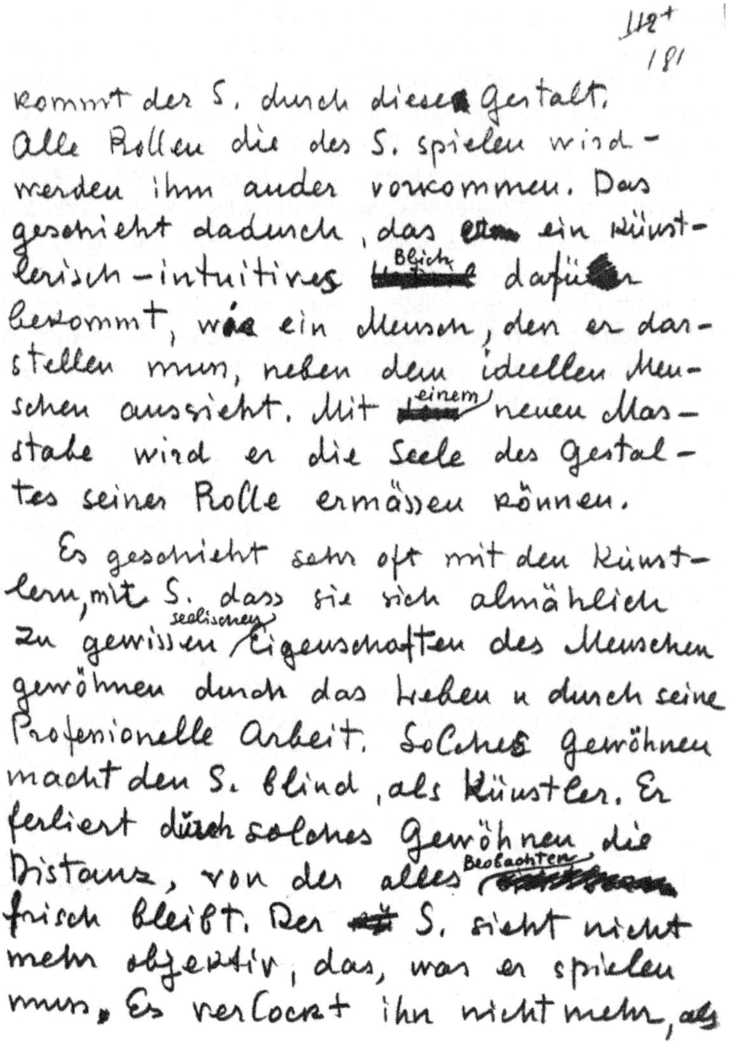

kommt der S. durch diese Gestalt.
Alle Rollen die des S. spielen wird –
werden ihm ander vorkommen. Das
geschieht dadurch, das ~~etwa~~ ein Künst-
lerisch-intuitives ~~Urteil~~ Blick dafür
bekommt, wie ein Mensch, den er dar-
stellen muss, neben dem ideellen Menschen aussieht. Mit ~~~~ einem neuen Mas-
stabe wird er die Seele des Gestaltes seiner Rolle ermässen können.

Es geschieht sehr oft mit den Künst-
lern, mit S. dass sie sich almählich
zu gewissen seelischen Eigenschaften des Menschen
gewöhnen durch das Leben u durch seine
Professionelle Arbeit. Solches gewöhnen
macht den S. blind, als Künstler. Er
verliert ~~durch solches~~ Gewöhnen die
Distanz, von der alles ~~Beobachten~~
frisch bleibt. Der ~~~~ S. sieht nicht
mehr objektiv, das, was er spielen
muss. Es verlockt ihn nicht mehr, als

FIGURE 23 *Page 181 of the 'Paris Manuscript'.*

A Path – First Stage

A path for the author's Work

Now let us follow the way in which the author's literary Work, available to the director and actors in the form of a book, passes along a complex and subtle path until it is finally transformed into a theatrical performance. Let us see how the director and actors are able to penetrate the author's Idea through the imaginary entities of the author's Work, gradually finding a purely *geistig* Idea, grasping it individually and appropriating it, then through the world of the imagination, the purely *geistig* is condensed into imaginary *Gestalten* that are wholly theatrical forms, leading finally to embodiment. Thus the literary form of the author's Idea is replaced by a theatrical form embodied through the power of acting, the living artistic word, scenery with its forms and colours, lighting etc. – all this will give the Idea body and a performance will emerge. The theatrical performance is an independent being. It is closely related to the literary being of the author's play, but it is far from being the same. Among the paths the Idea goes down from book to the stage, we can distinguish four stages. The actors and director must be familiar with these stages, so that the process of embodiment can proceed normally, organically and preferably undisturbed. Here one should already state that during the work the borders between these stages shouldn't be marked too pedantically or sharply. There are no such lines. These stages are the ground rules of human creativity, they have been inferred from the creative *Seele* and must help actors, rather than disturb them or make them pedantic. The stages must bring security and lead us to freedom.

The first stage begins with the author's play being read aloud, a delicate process that carries great responsibility. The reading aloud of the play is to give actors the first impression, which is of vital importance for the entire upcoming work by the actors, and something that will later be absorbed by their *Seele* and body. This is the moment of 'conception', as Stanislavski used to put it. The play will either be absorbed with interest and love, thereby making the actors' further work especially productive, or this doesn't occur. However, this often doesn't depend on the play, but rather on the manner in which the play is read aloud. While in other arts artists are able to work in isolation, the moment of the joint reading aloud is different. Artists who find their ideas and condense them in *Gestalten* of the imagination in complete isolation, suddenly and unexpectedly encounter their Idea and their visible and audible *Gestalten*. They receive their artistic Idea with such *seelisch* care, as delicately, as soft and lovingly as they like, as they are able. We have the testimony of many artists saying how important this moment is for everything that follows, for all further creative work. We know how many great artists kept their secret, their first love, to themselves, until they found the corresponding form to reveal this secret. Goethe, for instance, tells us this himself: 'I carried everything about with me in silence, and usually nothing was known to any one till the whole thing was complete. When I showed Schiller my "Hermann and Dorothea" finished, he was astonished, for I had said not a syllable to him of any such plan.' (Eckermann. Conversations with Goethe. 14 November 1923) Lone artists can do this. Much more care must be taken by actors, because for the most we part have no such aloneness.

The reading aloud of the play should be conducted by the director, who must make careful preparations. Certain demands will be made, and during the reading there must not be excessive intonation and nuance of the parts or characterization; no special emphasis or interpretation of the play should be made. Funny sections must not be read in a comical way, nor tragic sections tragically; the comical or tragic effect must come through the text, rather than the type of reading. In other words: the director must not, so to speak, act the play, just read it aloud. The reading aloud should be calm, slow, clear, intelligible, lucid, and preferably beautiful. Everything heard must immediately be imagined pictorially by the actors, and during the reading aloud they observe the entire play. The ideal situation would be for the actors to make their initial acquaintance with the play in the world of the imagination, through this reading aloud, but even if they already know the play they must create images in precisely the same way. Old, well-known plays must be read aloud and listened to as if for the first time.

One of the most important tasks of the method being suggested here is to prevent the actors from coming into contact with the intellect's abstract thinking. The artist's nature requires them to remain always in their element, in other words in the world of the imagination, during this work. All thinking that is needed during the work must be formed precisely as described previously: it must proceed through images. With experience and patient practice this can become a habit. Abstract, intellectual thinking must be a matter of the actors' will. It must not invade the actors' work against their will. The first reading aloud and listening to the play is precisely the moment in which a cold, abstract grasping by those listening can be tremendously harmful for all the work that is in store for the actors. The reading aloud can also be disturbed if the actors know <u>beforehand</u> how the parts are to be distributed, since they then instinctively acquire a certain artistic blindness for the rest of the play. As they observe, their own part will move into the foreground and hence leave their vision of the whole play incomplete, so it would be helpful, whenever possible, to distribute the parts after the collective reading aloud.

During this reading the actors first come into contact with the world of the imagination. They must strive to always remain – until a certain moment that will be described in the third stage – in the world of the imagination, and to engage more and more with the *Gestalten*, and the sounds, rhythms and atmospheres of this world. We shall see how this is possible in practice.

Penetrating the author's Idea

Now the actors begin to work specifically with the help of the *Gestalten* of the imagination. These *Gestalten* are formed by the actors in such a way that they correspond to the *Gestalten* of the author's text. The actors penetrate the region of the imagination where the author also observed and heard his or her *Gestalten*. The *Gestalten* the actors see are naturally not the same as those seen by the author during the writing of the play. But this is not at all necessary. What matters is that the actors receive the impulse from the author. This impulse turns the actors' gaze in a certain <u>direction</u>. This direction is such that it guides actors to the author's <u>artistic Idea</u>. The *Gestalten* seen by the actors during the reading aloud are similar and close to those of the author. The actors thereby penetrate the <u>root</u> of these *Gestalten*, the play's element – the <u>author's Idea</u>.

So in the first stage the actors needn't start their work rationalizing the author's Idea and fixing it in a logical form. That would make the Idea mental, dry, intellectual, abstract. And this would have a harmful effect. We must begin by using our artistic feelings to 'fore-feel', 'fore-sense' the author's Idea. The readings proceed with the actors observing the whole play afresh, until they have in their mind's eye images before them. During this repeated paying attention, the fore-feeling and fore-sensing of the play's Idea (that unites all *Gestalten* and gives them meaning) becomes more and more clear and lucid.

Signs of the play's Idea

Now we must clarify what we actually mean by the play's Idea. In seeking the Idea, the actors will come across certain guidelines. When we have a theatrical play before us, we must first test whether the play contains a true artistic Idea, and to do this we can look for certain features, certain signs. If the play really is, or at least potentially so, broad enough to hold an artistic Idea, then we will find three definite features that confirm its presence. An Idea-carrying play will expand in three directions:

1) The first leads towards a *Weltempfindung*.
   Everything that takes place in the world, everything that can be taken as an artistic theme, an artistic event, can be presented in such a way that the *Weltempfindung* in relation to this theme, this event, is more or less perceptible. The *Weltempfindung* in a play doesn't depend on the theme, but rather the breadth and depth of the author's *Geist*. One can take a small, insignificant theme, and through the greatness of the author's *Geist* it can be permeated with a *Weltempfindung*. Or one might touch upon a great and complex problem, and nevertheless its presentation may be artistically narrow, so that the *Weltempfindung* can find no place there (merely biased, inartistic elements).

   Every artistic event that holds within it an Idea stands (in some form) in relation to the world. We are dealing here with a relationship, and not stating that 'worldly issues' need to be touched upon in the play. It does not matter how the *Weltempfindung* finds expression. Whether it is like God in the Prologue of *Faust*, or something we sense in the nature of the main character, as is the case in *Peer Gynt*, or in the entire atmosphere of a fairytale, these are already questions concerning artistic form, the garment, the shell, the 'visible' form given the *Weltempfindung*, which gives the play the breadth it needs in order to be able to carry within it an Idea.

In this regard *Othello*, to take an example, is a rather inauspicious play. Its central theme is too sharply limited by the world. The feeling of the hero's jealous love is endlessly <u>expanded</u> and analysed by the author, but in this <u>expansion</u> the boundaries of the feelings, the passion, the love, these are never <u>ruptured</u>. They find no path into the broader world. Here the analysis remains merely analysis, it doesn't synthesize anything with worldly forces. In *Faust*, on the other hand, we have quite a different case. We find Doctor Faust himself in such a state that his increased and enlarged <u>human</u> wisdom is tearing down the boundaries and finding the wisdom of the <u>world</u>.

So the *Weltempfindung* is one direction in which a theatrical play carrying an Idea must lean.

2) The character with its destiny presents the second direction.

We have already touched upon this theme from one angle, when we spoke about actors having to develop a sense of the character, their inner path and the direction of this path, that they must develop within themselves a sense of character destiny. Now we approach this from a different point of view and place the same demands on the author, on the play.

To be able to express the Idea in the play the author must depict a <u>significant</u> character, whether in a positive or negative sense. An insignificant character may also be depicted, and this too can have great meaning, but they must be <u>significant</u> through their insignificance. No stray, random characters may be shown on stage (something naturalism is always forced to do), they must always be a character <u>type</u>. Through the author's art they must be raised up to a type, in order to be capable of embodying an artistic Idea. For example, many modern dramas, especially in films, consist nearly always of these random, insignificant characters. A significant character type in a play must also, during a performance, <u>transform</u> through the play's inner (and outer) incidents and events, and consciously or subconsciously follow their inner path. To this end, in truly artistic plays, incidents and actions are present that allow the character to follow their inner path before the audience's eyes.

Again, although Othello is shown by the author to be a significant character type, it is in the sense that he has no relationship to the world: he represents an uncomfortable artistic form precisely in order to embody the Idea. Othello follows no inner path and doesn't transform himself during the play, unlike Doctor Faust, King Lear etc. If we put these alongside many random film heroes, we will recognize the latter as being nothing more than outlines; they are not types, have no free will, and also no destiny. All that happens to them is a meaningless <u>accident</u>, and instead of following an inner path they are forced from one episode to the next with inner rigidity and inflexibility.

In the end, a significant character type who follows their inner path before an audience must veer towards good or evil. All inner (and outer) events must have a direction, a meaning, and therefore the theme of character destiny emerges in the play, the theme of the wise command of a character. Where a character's destiny and free will meet in a theatrical play, an inner action develops, justifying the outer actions.

3) Is the play broad enough to be able to reveal its artistic themes through two contrary forces in conflict?
These forces are: good and evil in all possible forms. These may be <u>within</u> the characters themselves, as artistically distinctive typical figures (Macbeth, Claudius, the Maid of Orleans, Faust, Romeo, etc.), or <u>around</u> those characters (for instance Yago alongside Othello, Cordelia and the other sisters alongside King Lear, etc.),

or surrounding the characters as *Gestalten* of the imagination (as with Mephistopheles, Macbeth's witches and fairytale or mythical *Gestalten*), and even through clear, artistically strong, distinctive destinies, as in ancient Greek tragedies, for example.

These are all imperative requirements for every play hoping to embody an Idea, and they will give the play the necessary breadth.

Dynamic scheme

Through these three directions, an image comes to us of an endless dynamic force for all art containing an Idea (see drawing), and in the landscape between plays which hold Ideas and those that do not, lies a whole series of plays that to some degree lean towards an Idea.

With such plays, the actors' task and that of the director is to use every possibility to develop it so that the Idea contained within the play grows and comes to the fore. They must do their utmost to deepen the play through their understanding. They must, so to speak, idealize the play, something readily possible for actors and directors who carry within themselves a developed sense of the world of character, character destiny, and the ever-present forces of good and evil.

Now let us ask ourselves: what exactly is the play's Idea? It is a dynamic form, an empty form containing within it: the whole world, the entire past, present and future characters with their destinies, all good and evil, all inner paths, ascents and descents. It contains all. And therefore it is completely empty. This is how human beings and artists also sense it, a vast emptiness that remains so for as long as the artist stands before this allness, this whole, without noticing anything in particular, concrete, separate. Then, as soon as the artist does notice something separately, this empty dynamic form immediately starts to become filled. The artist's eye may notice in this vastness a concrete character type, with its destiny, that becomes linked to concrete forms of good and evil, with a concrete relationship to the world. These three concrete elements are observed by the

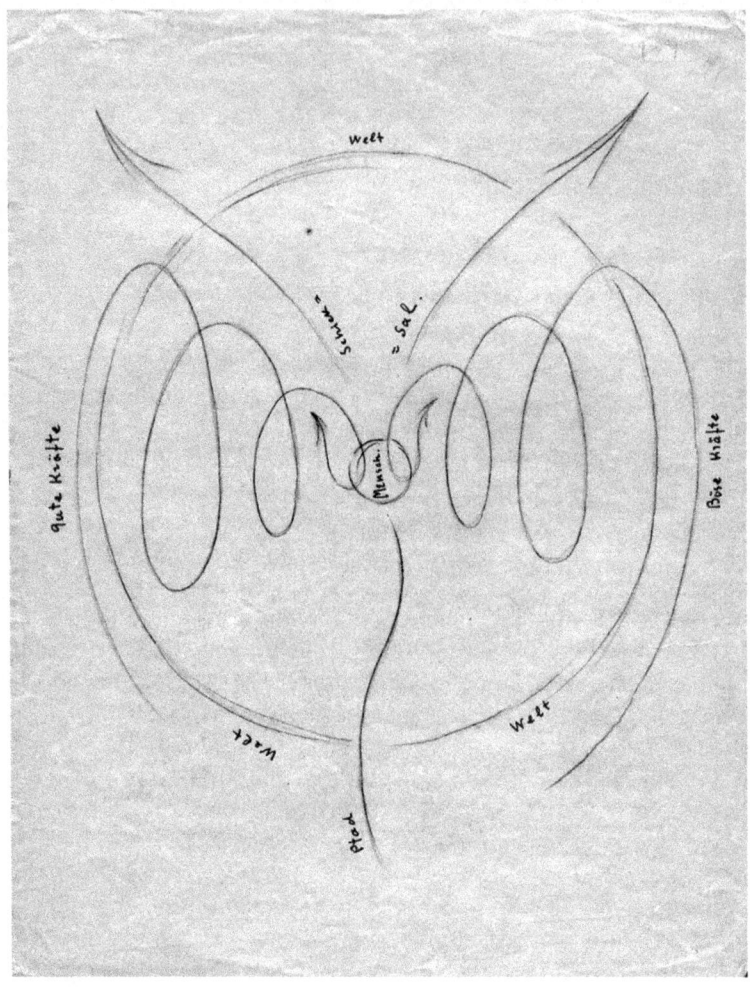

FIGURE 24 *Original diagram on page 207 of the 'Paris Manuscript'.*

[Translation: 'Pfad' = path; 'Welt' = world; 'Mensch' = humankind/character; 'Gute Kräfte' = good forces; 'Böse Kräfte' = evil forces; 'Schick ... sal' = destiny]

artist in the vastness and gradually become outlined, creating the form for the play's artistic Idea. Now, in order to able to be able to observe these three concrete elements, our 'eyes' must be open, by which we mean our awoken, wide-eyed individuality. When this particular combination of the three elements (world, character, force) is experienced and created by an author – one who is not a materialist – they represent the artistic form for the Idea and it receives from the artist its garment, a shell. Artistic *Gestalten*, atmospheres, rhythm, words etc. make up this body, shell, garment. The Idea becomes embodied. For the author the body is a <u>literary</u> one. As actors we find ourselves facing this literary body, the author's *Gestalten*, and our task now is to use them to penetrate the author's Idea. In order to test whether there truly is an Idea to be found beyond the *Gestalten*, we have this endlessly dynamic form at our disposal to detect and comprehend it.

In this period the actors often receive the loveliest inspirations that will later evolve and develop into wonderful particulars and details for the part. However these inspirations can easily be forgotten during the later stages of the work, therefore it is important that during this first stage each actor begin a journal. There is no need to put down extensive descriptions of our vision of the character, much less 'thoughts' about the play, rather the journal is simply for making short notes, perhaps drawn sketches, a word, a letter, whatever appears of real importance to the actors and gives them particular joy. These notes will be a great help later. Everything that was noted in the journal during the first phase will seem quite different and bring many new impulses to excite the imagination later on.

The Idea that the actors themselves create by means of the author's stimulation, won't be <u>exactly</u> the author's Idea. It will be observed, felt, experienced by the actors in <u>their own</u> way. And this is precisely the point, the author's Idea will be coloured by the actor's <u>individuality</u>. Perhaps in a theoretical, logical, abstract sense it will be the same Idea as the author's, yet in a practical, <u>artistic</u> sense it will be a differently coloured, individual *seelisch* Idea. It will <u>belong</u> to each actor, and that is the most important thing. Actors cannot truthfully and full-bloodedly represent someone else's Idea on stage, that would be psychologically impossible. Through an appropriation of the author's Idea, through this individual colouring of the Idea, actors fully acquire the right to experience the author's Idea as their own and represent it on stage. This occurs in each actor's *Seele*, and provided we become inwardly active in our seeking of the author's Idea in the three directions described above, it will quickly come within reach. In doing this, we need not embark on a discussion with the author. That is not the actors' task.

The actors now begin to see the play's *Gestalten* somewhat differently. During the first reading aloud of the play, before they knew the author's Idea, they observed them from below, so to speak. But now they have obtained a feeling for and grasp of the play, the same *Gestalten* are seen from above, from the world of the Idea. Of course, provisionally, all that can be seen from above is a shadowy, sketchy impression of the *Gestalten*, and the Idea itself is not fully experienced or felt right through, but in the first stage this is how it must be. Then, alongside the observation of *Gestalten* and through the seeking and appropriation of the play's Idea, the actors also try to experience a sense of the atmospheres. They run the whole play over again in their imaginations, and each time new discoveries will be made in relation to the Idea, *Gestalten* and atmospheres. Similarly, during the first stage a fore-sense of the play's rhythm should be sought, but not for individual scenes, or for the dialogue, monologues etc. It will suffice to sense the rhythmic differences between the tragic, dramatic, lyrical, humorous etc., to get a sense of the rhythmic nature of the author's text, but only in general terms. It may happen, however, that rhythmic details suddenly come into view in the actors' *Seele*, and these observations needn't be rejected, but for the time being there is no need for such details to actually be sought.

It should be stressed that what is being described here are simply a few laws of creation, a certain hygiene of creation, but it must all be taken very freely and used individually in practice. Only then will what is being suggested here make sense. From time to time, the actors take the play and read it through again, and here too seek to observe everything, hear everything, and fore-sense everything. They must resist the 'book', in other words fight their habit of rushing to 'understand' the printed page in an abstract way. All the material presented must be transformed in their imagination into an 'actable form'.

It is also desirable that before going to sleep in the evening the actors bring to life in their imaginations the *Gestalt* of their part and those of the other characters. The unconscious, or to be more precise, super-conscious, noble regions of the actor's *Seele* are always active during sleep, and it is here that the actor's individuality will be at work. It creates by itself and prepares the actor's future Work. The dreams of humankind and the creative act go beyond being merely related to each other, and actors must also develop the habit of observing their dreams upon waking. There is no need to analyse, interpret, or decipher them, something that would actually be harmful. No, it is just a matter of delving into the dreams, <u>observing</u> and <u>sensing</u>, for the dreams of humankind have the <u>style</u> of artistic <u>creation</u>. This is the main point, and therein lies the meaning of dreams for actors. Through the attentive recollection of our dreams, we gradually awaken in our *Seele* a refined sense that will show us the very nature of the <u>style of human creativity</u>.

The meaning of the first stage lies in the notion that the actors sense their future Work as a <u>whole</u>. Through properly conducted sessions for the reading aloud, the actors acquire a <u>need</u> to create, something actors must value and preserve. This can be achieved by not going too fast or going into details of the play, but rather by prolonging the experience of the <u>whole</u> and the activity of sensing. An <u>abundance</u>, a <u>richness</u> lies hidden within this still embryonic general <u>whole</u>, and actors who summon their feelings too soon and without harmony will soon tire and become bored by them. They will force these feelings into the text, whereas words that are first prepared by being artistically shaped will never be boring. On the contrary, only such words will truly be able to awaken artistic feelings in an actor's *Seele*, so actors must first concern themselves with the word by itself, with the tonal elements of their art, without killing the word through fake feelings. Feelings won't ever be killed by the artistic word, but the artistic word is always killed by fake, forced feelings.

It is in this stage that the actors <u>fall in love</u>, so to speak, with a living being that is at once near and far, although this will only come about through their creative work over time. The actors' first love of their future Work can quite correctly be compared to a mother's love for her child, during the period where the child still remains couched in that motherly love. A poet, for example, can sense more or less clearly during this period certain rhythms of a future poem, without knowing the content. Or a painter can get a foretaste of the colour and qualities of a painting, without knowing the theme. In this initial period of fore-sensing what is to come, the creative forces are gathered that are necessary for the work that lies before the actors and director. The first stage is one in which the director and actors breathe in the *seelisch* air.

We have said that the boundaries of the stages of the creative process are not sharp and clear. They flow into one another, and this is precisely the case here: everything described in the second stage will already have been gradually developing at the end of the first stage's feeling of the whole etc.

A Path – Second Stage

This begins with the <u>active observation</u> of the play by the director and actors together. Specific work begins on the play with systematic 'conversations' with the *Gestalten*, with the director and actors forming a connection with these *Gestalten* of the imagination as if they were living (in a sense independent) beings. They ask the *Gestalten* certain questions and wait for them to <u>answer</u> (whether immediately or only later). The questions put to the living *Gestalten* of the imagination (and across different parts of the play) arise from the joint work of the actors and director.

During the first stage, the actors and director have received a more or less clear <u>fore</u>-sense of the play's Idea, so the process of the <u>independent</u>, new creation of this Idea has already begun. Now this process of grasping and assimilating the Idea goes further. It is the Idea that guides the process of questioning, with the character answering from the world of *Gestalten*, but meanwhile the Idea will itself become increasingly clear and lucid and acquire a certain colouring, always corresponding to the inner character of the group undertaking the work. It is desirable for the actors to carry out the process of asking questions themselves alone, while during collective rehearsals it is the director that leads the process of questioning, and they must prepare this work in such a way that all questions may be answered through <u>observing</u>, through <u>images</u>. The director puts each question in turn, the actors listen and look for the answers in the world of *Gestalten*. They <u>observe</u> the answer. They shouldn't seek to answer the director's questions by reasoning, that would be useless and fail to nourish the actors' artistic *Seele* or awaken any artistic impulses. Rather than merely understand anything mentally, the actors strive to observe the answer in a scenic image and hence <u>feel</u> it.

The questions that are put to the world of *Gestalten* may fall into seven groups, or themes:

1) *Weltempfindung*
2) Character and character destiny
3) Forces of good and evil
4) Atmosphere
5) The substance, the play's 'what', its events

6) The characters' actions
7) The composition of the characters

The purpose of putting questions in these seven directions is the complete discovery of the play's Idea, its embodiment on stage with a clear, true rhythmic form. Let us review these themes:

1) *Weltempfindung.*
Every play, in accordance with its Idea, carries its own characteristic *Weltempfindung*, which is decidedly different in *Hamlet*, *King Lear*, *Faust*, *Peer Gynt* etc. Through posing questions to the world of the imagination, we must discover, become familiar with and feel our way into the play's *Weltempfindung* as deeply as we can, for it would be highly inartistic to present *Hamlet* with the same *Weltempfindung* as *Faust*, for instance, or to pay no attention to it at all, since without grasping and sensing the play's characteristic *Weltempfindung* we will never penetrate its deepest layers. The entire cast must be able to carry this *Weltempfindung* in their *Seele* and radiate it, regardless of which part they are playing, which words they speak during the performance.

<u>All</u> engage with the will of the entire performance, and have no exclusively personal tasks or goals; a single goal unites them all, being the harmony of the whole performance. From this point of view, there are no greater or smaller parts, nobody without responsibility. Everyone in the play, even if they don't speak a word on stage, can make the performance harmonious or discordant. For instance, a dreadful disharmony can occur on stage when the main character is forced to <u>alone</u> express the play's meaning and depth. None of the meaning and depth of the author's words will be of any help if they are spoken in a disharmonious environment.

One might respond: 'Hamlet carries a *Weltempfindung* within him, and speaks such great and meaningful words about the world and humankind, but other characters in *Hamlet* have no real humanity or *Weltempfindung*. For example, Rosenkrantz and Guildenstern, who negate the world with their whole being, why do such characters need to develop a *Weltempfindung* during rehearsals?'

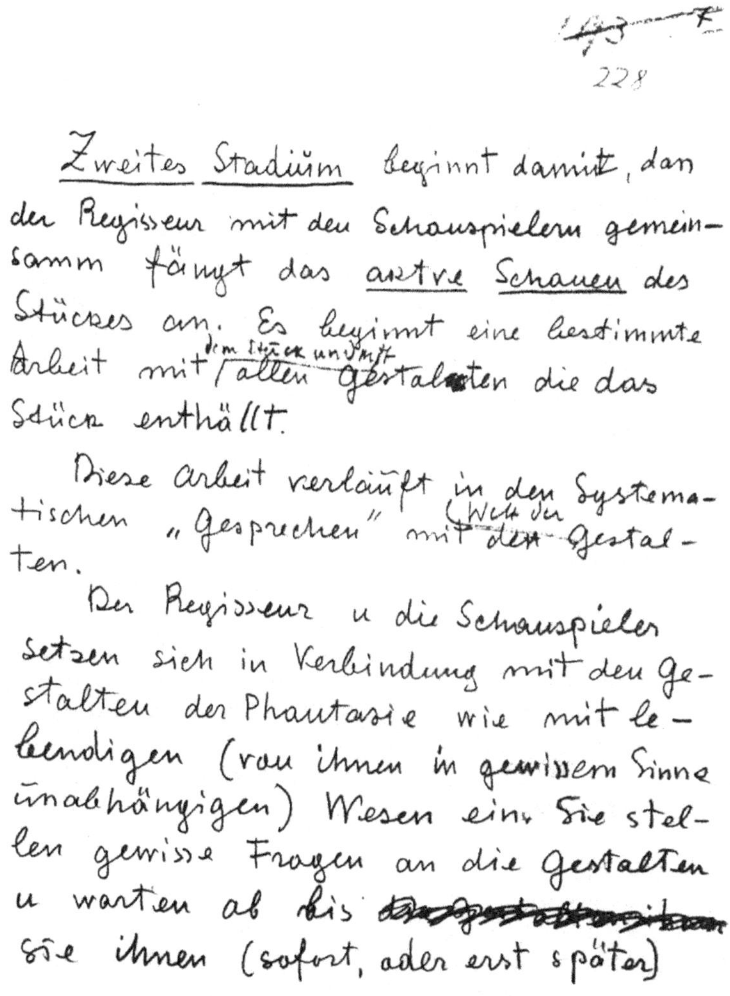

228

<u>Zweites Stadium</u> beginnt damit, dass der Regisseur mit den Schauspielern gemeinsamm fängt das aktive Schauen des Stückes an. Es beginnt eine bestimmte Arbeit mit dem Stück und mit /allen Gestalten die das Stück enthällt.

Diese Arbeit verläuft in den Systematischen „Gesprechen" mit (Welt der) Gestalten.

Der Regisseur u die Schauspieler setzen sich in Verbindung mit den Gestalten der Phantasie wie mit lebendigen (von ihnen in gewissem Sinne unabhängigen) Wesen ein. Sie stellen gewisse Fragen an die Gestalten u warten ab bis ~~dnwwwwwwww~~ sie ihnen (sofort, oder erst später)

FIGURE 25 *Page 228 of the 'Paris Manuscript'.*

We must answer this as follows: we cannot portray characters that negate the world if we as <u>actors</u> aren't familiar with the play's *Weltempfindung*, if we don't know what is involved in our characters. How can we as <u>artists</u> say 'no' to the world, if we don't know the 'world' of the play? We will find no proper expression to this 'no', it will be empty and feelingless. Artists can only find a dark colour properly and <u>convincingly</u> if they know the light colours, and vice versa.

2) Character and character destiny.
Although actors must make their character a significant, typical *Gestalt*, no thought should be given to which <u>type</u> this or that character is, rather this must be observed. A sense of the <u>wise</u> command of the character through their destiny helps them experience the inner path of their part as a <u>complete</u> artistic and, we might say, musical theme. The actors see the play's Idea from a distinct angle, and this Idea will in turn make the characters' destinies appropriate and meaningful.

3) Forces of good and evil.
Through this type of study of the play's forces and their preparatory work (see the essay Artistic Individuality), the actors and director will fashion such forces on stage, thereby lifting the entire performance high above the level of naturalism. It will no longer please them artistically to do such things by halves, and they will feel how strongly the play's Idea is expressed, whenever its forces of good and evil are strongly pronounced.

4) Atmosphere.
The play has a <u>main atmosphere</u>, which we must similarly learn to sense through observation. It will depend on several points: whether it is a tragedy, comedy, drama, fairytale, satire etc., a modern or old play, whether the story takes place in this or that period of time, written by this or that author, and so on. Meanwhile, the performance itself gets its special atmosphere through the *Weltanschauung* developed by the actors and director, based on the play's Idea.

The general main atmosphere always remains tragic, dramatic, fantastic fairytale-like, or humorous <u>as a whole</u>, as a key signature, the musical key in which the play will be performed, while the play will also have smaller atmospheres that follow on from one another, can fight each other, transform themselves, unite etc. There must never be an instant on stage without atmosphere. The main atmosphere and the smaller atmospheres must be clearly found by the director and actors, and must represent the performance's '*seelisch*-musical' <u>score</u>.

5) The substance, the play's 'what', its events.
The fifth group deals with the event (both outer and inner) as described by the author. This event is a garment, a shell, an outer form for the Idea that the author wishes to bring to expression. To a greater or lesser degree, it will be a complex composition made up of smaller events following on from one another, all pursuing one single goal: to reveal, express and make understandable the play's Idea; pictorially, vividly.

6) The characters' actions
The play's plot drives the characters, and each character has their will, each pursues an objective. Out of these a plot objective, a will current emerges flowing through the play. Just as the whole play must be seen as a unified event, so too this current of the will should be seen and felt as a unifying current of energy. In order to be able to observe this, we concentrate our attention on the characters' will and actions, watching the whole play over again in our imagination and paying attention to the main action and overall will arising from each character's will.

And here a particular point must be observed: the play is <u>one</u> event divided into several events following on from one another, but with the play's will stream there are from the start <u>two</u> streams, two actions, both of which are in opposition: action and a counter-action, will and counter-will.

These opposing actions fight each other and it is precisely this <u>struggle</u> that forms the play's will stream.

Again, the action and its counter-action must be discovered by observation, which is how we grasp the play's Idea as expressed through the characters' actions and each counter-action.

Here we must be able to clearly differentiate between an action or objective that is merely <u>understood</u> by the actors, and one that is observed <u>pictorially</u>. 'Hamlet wants to destroy King Claudius'. This we can know. This is not correct for an actor. One must imagine pictorially <u>how</u> Hamlet destroys King Claudius. We must imagine this as clearly as possible and then the <u>image</u> itself will show actors the right way as they rehearse. Actors must always live in <u>images</u>. The images are the <u>living artistic</u> impulses of creation. Our reason, on the other hand, is a dead, inartistic substance with which we can do nothing. Actors must <u>comprehend</u> what they do, but only afterwards, based on whatever their artistic feelings have prescribed and that the imagination has shown through images. We may take into consideration the suggestions of the mind, but these are only impulses that <u>give direction</u>, and should not represent a force <u>replacing the imagination</u>. Our reason is perfectly capable of giving actors <u>direction and suggestions</u>, but it is in no way a <u>creative</u> force, and all of the characters' single actions and objectives must be discovered by the actors through observation, and then set in images.

7) The composition of the play's characters.
All parts, all characters in the play are presented by the author with a particular aim, namely the visual shaping of the Idea. It follows that all the play's characters have been considered by the author as a collective <u>composition</u>. For actors this means we cannot develop our own part in isolation, but must study the *Gestalten* of the other characters just as carefully. In order to achieve this composition, we ask ourselves: which characters carry the play's action and which the counter-action?

Initially we discover two groups of characters and observe that those with similar objectives are nevertheless different. For example, no two evil characters in the play are portrayed the same. On the contrary: they must be seen and presented as differently as possible, in order to be able to show the image of evil in the play from as many angles as possible.

    The questioning of the world of *Gestalten* continues during the second stage, and although this must be systematic, the questions should not be grouped pedantically. Arbitrary questions may be put in any desired order, according to whatever interests the director or the actors at any given moment. We must also be aware that it is always possible for the character's *Gestalt* to reveal themselves suddenly to the actor, but <u>not</u> in answer to a question put by the actor or director. We must gratefully receive any such independent manifestation of the *Gestalt*, and allow the *Gestalten* to come forward quite freely, to reveal themselves. Whenever the actors expect something in line with a specific question, but notice that instead the *Gestalt* shows something quite different, we simply allow the *Gestalt* to take the lead, retract our question, wait and observe.

    Now the director and actors have a more or less clear picture of the elements of the future performance, namely: *Weltempfindung*, character and their destiny, the forces of good and evil, the score of atmospheres, the score of events, the will stream of actions, composition of the characters, and sounds. And we must speak of another important aspect to our observations in the imagination. Let us recall that observing the outer *Gestalt* is at the same time the observation of their inner life, and through practice and experience actors know that all they observe of the outer *Gestalt* is merely a manifestation, a concentration, of the inner. And that the inner is the *Seele* of the observed outer. Now let us ask ourselves, what is it exactly to observe the inner? To observe the *Gestalt*'s *Seele* means both to empathize <u>with</u> and have compassion <u>for</u> the *Gestalt*, for the character. We laugh or cry with our character's *Gestalt*, we suffer or rejoice <u>with</u> their sufferings and joys, and through our love we find the power of empathy. Meanwhile, the power of love, of empathy, that an actor has in life, as a person, will affect how deep or superficial, fine or coarse, original or banal these observations will be.

    As we observe the *Gestalt*'s *Seele*, we should remain quite <u>objective</u>, having no personal (naturalistic) <u>experience</u> of what is seen in the *Gestalt*'s *Seele*. Empathy means to feel <u>with</u> the *Gestalt*, and empathetic objectivity forms better 'eyes' with which to observe than any personal, 'real' <u>experience</u> coloured by egotism. The true artist always remains <u>above</u> their creation during the whole process. We may call this work carried out by the actors: <u>rehearsing and playing in the world of the imagination</u>. That is the most important element of the second stage, to prepare the entire performance in our *Geist*. Undisturbed by all that is personal, we can freely view with <u>empathy</u> the entire domain of our creation. All personal experience that gets mixed in with our work will result in something heavy and limited, while objective, empathetic love, on the other hand, gives the creation an artistic lightness and breadth.

One may ask: what is the difference between our personal feelings and what is described here as objective empathy (feeling <u>with</u>)? Everything that we experience in our life personally, <u>directly</u>, the feelings, thoughts and will impulses, still have strong ties to our lower ego, to egotism. These direct *Seele* experiences are not yet 'artistic material'. Through <u>forgetting</u>, our direct, egotistically lived experiences are able to sink into the unconscious regions of our *Seele*, where they follow complex paths and only resurface later, transformed. But now they are no longer egotistical and personal, they have become objective and can be used as 'artistic material'. When actors prepare their role, they have to awaken within themselves these unconsciously transformed feelings. This can be done in two ways.

Here is one way: the actors take their part and observe which feelings are contained therein, working themselves up for as long as it takes for them to personally get these feelings themselves. They take their part to be a real, egotistical personal experience, and strive to make the e.g. anger, hatred, fright, despair, weeping, and so on, genuine. This can be achieved, although other feelings such as love, admiration, devotion, amazement, as well as humour, joy etc., are much harder to find using this method. Once they have worked up these experiences and will impulses within themselves, the feelings may endure, and the actor, being by now tired, weak and drained, may even experience a whiff of objective empathy and transformed feelings. But this will never be more than a <u>whiff</u> and must always be a matter of chance. They can also do as follows: they seek in their own recollections some

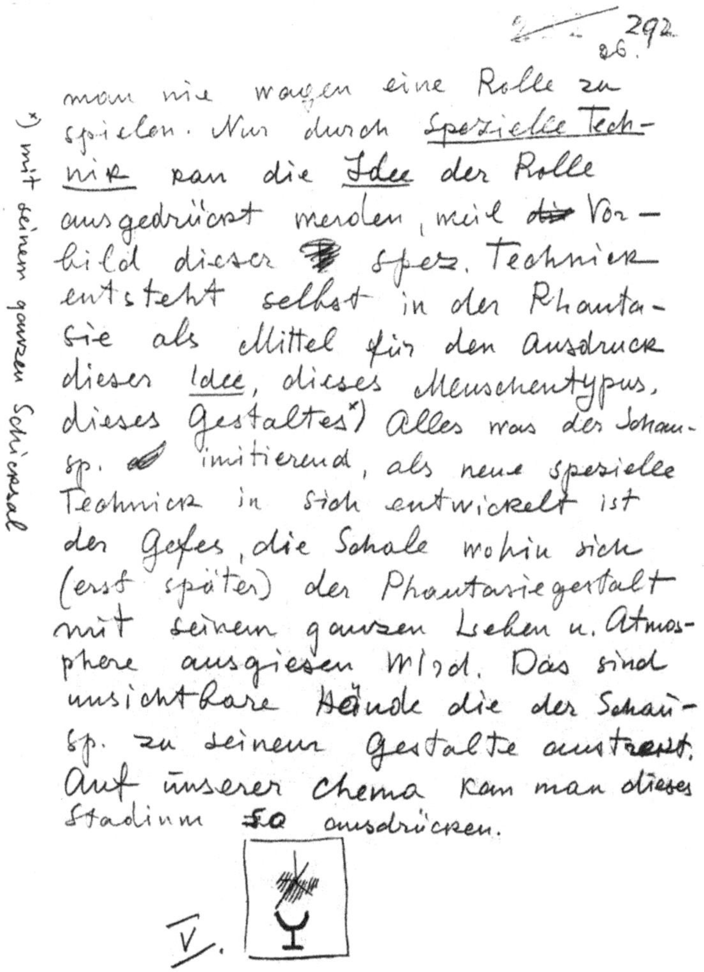

292
26.

man nie wagen eine Rolle zu spielen. Nur durch spezielle Technik kan die Idee der Rolle ausgedrückt werden, weil Vorbild dieser spez. Technik entsteht selbst in der Phantasie als Mittel für den Ausdruck dieser Idee, dieses Menschentypus, dieses Gestaltes*) Alles was der Schausp. imitierend, als neue spezielle Technik in sich entwickelt ist der Gefäs, die Schale wohin sich (erst später) der Phantasiegestalt mit seinem ganzen Leben u. Atmosphere ausgiesen wird. Das sind unsichtbare Hände die der Schausp. zu seinem Gestalte anstreckt. Auf unserer Schema kann man dieses Stadium so ausdrücken.

V.

*) mit seinem ganzen Schicksal

FIGURE 26 *Page 292 of the 'Paris Manuscript'.*

experiences corresponding to the role and then work themselves up through their memories. It doesn't make much difference. Either way, the experiences will remain personal.

What happens to the author's Work in this case, to the characters the author has imagined and described? They remain in the 'book', rather than becoming embodied. The actors perform with their own everyday feelings and emotions, instead of revealing the feelings of the characters as described by the author. In such methods in which the real experiences of the actors are used, the actors have nothing more at their disposal, beyond their own everyday emotions. They cannot, for instance, hate as King Claudius hates, be jealous as Othello, love as Romeo does, sacrifice themselves as the Maid of Orleans. At best what they'll manage is simply what they themselves would do in everyday life, although perhaps in a more intense fashion (in other words: 'spirited'), and in the same order as given by the author. That is one way that actors may perhaps, by chance, be able to get through to objective feelings that have ceased to be personal.

But there is another way, in which the actor is guided directly to the transformed feelings that have been turned into 'artistic material', and it is this: the actors objectively observe the inner and outer image of their part. Observing the image in the imagination awakens in the actors' *Seele* the feelings that have already been transformed by the unconscious regions of the *Seele*. These gradually form around the *Gestalt* and over time increase more and more. The actors leave their personal, everyday feelings untouched. Such feelings remain quite still and don't interfere with the work of observing. An artist's, an actor's transformed feelings are altogether different from those that we know in everyday life. They are far broader, more beautiful and varied than commonplace ones. They are subtler and wiser. Why is this so? Because the unconscious process of transformation is guided by the actor's individuality. The individuality of the higher consciousness will, by transforming feelings, supply us with purified and wise forces. The transformed, purified feelings that gather around the *Gestalt* and that reverberate as empathy in the actor's *Seele*, will later form the character's feelings. And whenever the part is truly, so to speak, hygienically prepared in this way, it can come about that actors truly experience the character, not with their usual, everyday feelings, but rather with transformed, 'artistic' feelings and will impulses.

Soon after the *Gestalt* has revealed themselves, the actor may begin to observe their own self beside the *Gestalt* and ask: what through my work can I change within myself so that the character's *Gestalt* retains as many of their traits as possible, and I be led as far as possible away from my own habits? This striving by actors with each new character, to change <u>themselves</u> ever more, is the only true possibility for development and advancement in our profession. Very often, what we commonly refer to as development and experience is in reality nothing more than a collection of physical and *seelisch* habits, which although over time do facilitate the actor's work, render them mere artisans repeating themselves over and over. The author's *Gestalten* and ideas play an ever more secondary role, until they no longer have any meaning for the actor, being thereby also lost to audiences, who are forced to watch and listen to the same actor over and over, just with, at the most, a different mask and different words. During an actor's work adapting to the character's *Gestalt*, it will <u>itself</u> change as it seeks the paths allowing it to become embodied through the actor. Thus the *Gestalt* also acquires its own new imprint, and the more intensively actors work on the characters in the realm of the imagination, the more this magical world will help us and present a whole multitude of different variations of our newly minted *Gestalt*. The development of the *Gestalten* by the actors and the whole play by the director in the realm of the imagination, heralds the end of the second stage.

The actors now see their *Gestalten* outwardly and inwardly, they hear them, know their physical, *seelisch* and speech traits, they know the play's Idea, have each developed in their *Seele* a shared experience of and empathy for their *Gestalt*, a sense of the score of atmospheres for the play and their part, and they have also found out a great deal about the rhythmic forms. They are now able to play everything through in their imaginations, not just elements directly linked to their part, but also other sections in the play. During the second stage, the director too has achieved much in relation to the play and its composition, having created the whole performance in their imagination. As before, the second stage gradually merges into the third.

A Path – Third Stage

So far the actors have worked only in the world of the imagination. The *Gestalt* of their part was there, but they themselves were here, separate from each other. Now, very carefully and patiently, they begin to embody. How does this happen? They try to imitate the *Gestalt*. For instance, they see a certain movement and do the same movement for as long as it takes for this movement to correspond to their imagined *Gestalt*. They hear the *Gestalt*'s voice and try to repeat this voice. When we recall that for actors everything outer in the *Gestalt* is merely a sign of the inner, we may understand that in imitating the *Gestalt* we must imitate the inner, the *Gestalt*'s *Seele* through the outer form. We will sense a strong physical resistance, so we begin with whatever we see the clearest. It is a long process that demands a great deal of caution and patience.

During the third stage, the imitation of parts of the *Gestalt* gather in the actors' body with a wholeness (for the director this occurs with the entire play). The actors gradually find the corresponding form to be embodied, and this work is nothing other than the training of a special technique that emerges for this part alone. All the characteristic traits that the actor acquires for this part during the imitation are special. These must be so well rehearsed and penetrate the actor's body and *Seele* so deeply, that they truly form a technique for this character, and we should never be so bold as to play a character with our general technique alone; the part's Idea (the imagined human type, the *Gestalt* and its destiny) can only find expression through a special technique. Everything that actors imitate, being a new special technique developed within, is the vessel, the cup into which (only later) the imagined *Gestalt* with their entire life and atmosphere will be poured. We stretch out invisible hands towards our *Gestalt*, and this stage can be further expressed in our diagram. (Figure V). However, the *Gestalt* doesn't come to the actor immediately, but rather remains separate until through the special technique we become organically united, our body and voice etc., until we feel quite light, flexible and free within this new technique.

Let us try to describe how rehearsals should proceed in this phase, but again, we shouldn't take these progressions too pedantically. Initially, the actors 'tell' their director what has been observed and perceived in the world of the *Gestalten*. This 'telling' is completely wordless, with each actor playing for the director everything they have observed in the imagination, the *Gestalten*, atmospheres, rhythms great and small. It makes absolutely no difference in which order this occurs and the director forms their own image of all this, in addition to their own idea of the forthcoming performance, of the composition of the whole. Although they have been working together throughout, there will nevertheless be many differences between what the director 'sees' and the sketches the actors now play, and he or she watches quite openly and without bias. Following this, the director can unite their own imagination with those of the actors and, as has already been mentioned, a trait of all *Gestalten* is to unify, so the director now seeks the resulting synthesis. The actors too observe what their partners have shown, allowing them to picture each other's imaginations ever more precisely.

Let us now briefly review the situation in which these collaborating artists now find themselves. They have at their disposal a series of elements from which the performance can emerge. How have these elements been received? They have been gradually received through observation, from all that in the first reading aloud was anticipated ('fore-felt') and embryonic. From that point onwards, all the work carried out has been analytical, but the analysis has always been achieved by purely artistic means using a purely artistic method. This analysis, as described here, has killed nothing in the director's and actors' *Seele*. The individual elements of the whole now lie before the collaborating artists as living beings with a desire and the ability to become organic, harmonious, rhythmical syntheses. These individual elements are:

1) The play's Idea.
2) The *Weltanschauung* of those working on this Idea.
3) The *Weltempfindung* in the play.
4) The character with its destiny.
   a) The character's personality.
   b) This character as human type.
   c) The character's path (transformation).
   d) The direction of the inner path.

5) The opposing (good and evil) forces affecting the play.
6) The play's atmospheres.
7) The events of the play.
8) The will stream (actions of the character) in the play.
9) The composition of the characters.
10) Speech formation.

Now that the analysis has been accomplished, the synthesis may proceed and must be equally artistic, in order to attain the highest level. At each stage, the director and actors must be free in their work and the material remain loose and flexible. The <u>search</u> itself must give them artistic pleasure, rather than there being a sportsperson's sense of a final goal. Although the actors have already penetrated far into the world of the imagination, nevertheless we must still take care not to allow the intellect's habit of abstract thinking to get the upper hand. Work on the play may thus proceed, systematically, scene by scene, from beginning to end. Rehearsing in this way will gradually lead to the building up of an organic, artistic synthesis of all these elements in the actors' *Seele*. The further the work advances, the larger the sections of the play the director is able facilitate, until finally, and again completely organically, the need arises to present the entire play, with the whole *mise-en-scène*, in rhythmic form, on stage. The actors are now sufficiently sure of the world of the imaginary *Gestalten* that they can observe their characters easily and clearly in all possible situations, and are now approaching the happiest moment, when the character is embodied by their body and *Seele*.

They may now turn their attention to the <u>outer world</u>. Up to this point they have been enriching themselves through their imaginations only, and now they do so further through occasional impressions from what is seen, a person, an animal, a flower, these may provide interesting or meaningful new brushstrokes for the character. Different life situations, different atmospheres that they come across may speak to them, they start to notice unexpected, noteworthy, expressive rhythms that hadn't been perceived before, and all this enriches them further. They see small individual 'traits' of the outer world quite differently, as if with new eyes, and all that is observed gathers in their *Seele* as nourishment for their creativity, for their character. Through the <u>outer</u> world, they now see the <u>inner</u> world.

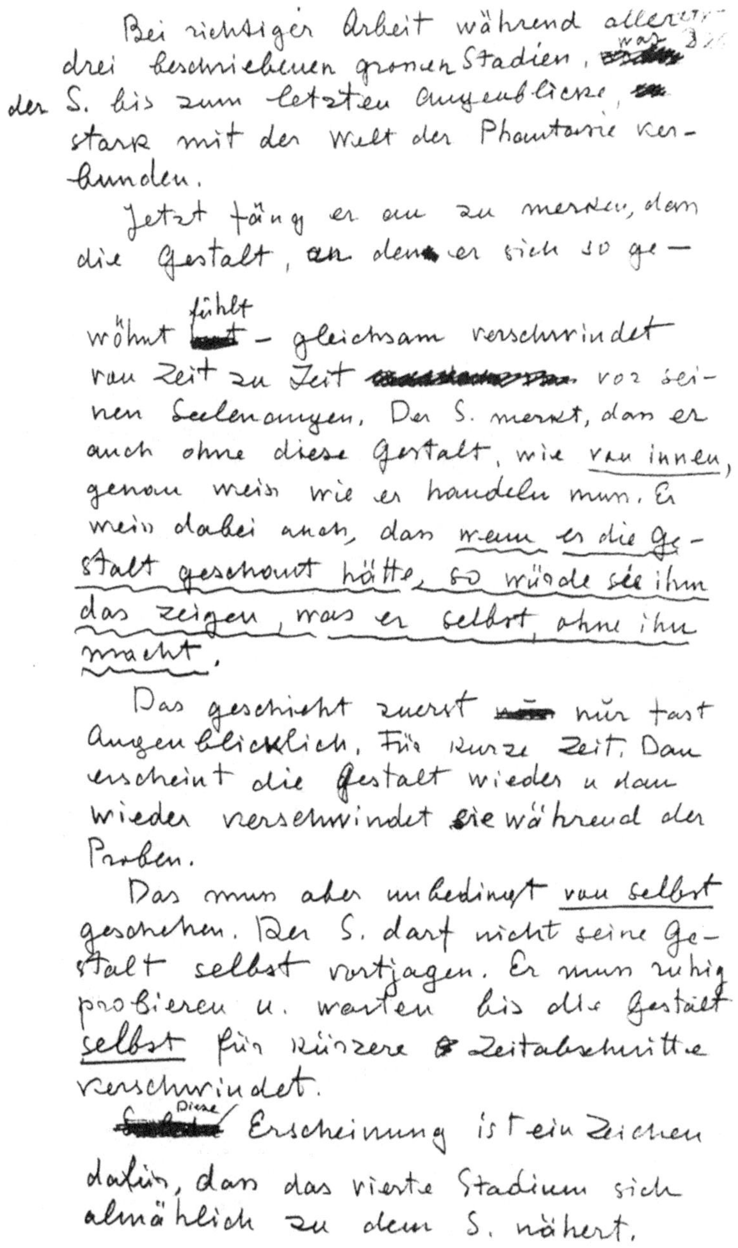

Bei richtiger Arbeit während aller
drei beschriebenen großen Stadien, war
der S. bis zum letzten Augenblicke,
stark mit der Welt der Phantasie verbunden.

Jetzt fängt er an zu merken, dass
die Gestalt, an den er sich so ge-
wöhnt fühlt — gleichsam verschwindet
von Zeit zu Zeit vor sei-
nen Seelenaugen. Der S. merkt, dass er
auch ohne diese Gestalt, wie von innen,
genau weiss wie er handeln muss. Er
weiss dabei auch, dass wenn er die Gestalt geschaut hätte, so würde sie ihm
das zeigen, was er selbst ohne ihn
macht.

Das geschieht zuerst nur fast
augenblicklich. Für kurze Zeit. Dann
erscheint die Gestalt wieder u dann
wieder verschwindet sie während der
Proben.

Das muss aber unbedingt von selbst
geschehen. Der S. darf nicht seine Gestalt selbst vorjagen. Er muss ruhig
probieren u. warten bis die Gestalt
selbst für kürzere Zeitabschnitte
verschwindet.

Diese Erscheinung ist ein Zeichen
dafür, dass das vierte Stadium sich
allmählich zu dem S. nähert.

FIGURE 27 Page 329 of the 'Paris Manuscript'.

Why has this come about? Because they now have the eye to observe. This eye is: the character itself. They see the character through the outer world. They see in the world <u>that which</u> the character needs in order to be enriched. This is the greatest prize that artists receive from their creative activity: they constantly see the world differently, always from another aspect, always with different eyes, according to whichever Idea they are embodying at each moment. In other words, they now observe as an <u>individuality</u>, as the representative of a *Weltanschauung*. One may ask, why didn't the actors already do this previously, if it can so enrich their part? Because initially they had no eye for the outer world and would have been in the same situation as a naturalistic actor. Naturalistic actors take external signs from the outer world and merely copy them in accordance with how they see the part. But because they have no inner structure for the part, no Idea guiding them, it doesn't matter to them what an outer sign means inwardly. They don't delve <u>deep</u> into the inner meaning of the outer, and they thereby remove the possibility of creating something different, deeper, that comes from <u>within</u>. The more such actors copy the outer world, the poorer they become in relation to inner possibilities. It is quite different for an actor who creates <u>first</u> in the world of the imagination, and <u>then</u> turns to the outer world. The inner depths reached through this work in the world of the imagination also reveal the <u>depths</u> of the outer world.

With correct work during all three of the stages as described so far, the actors have right up to the present moment been strongly connected to the world of the imagination. Now they start to notice that from time to time the *Gestalt*, with which they have become so familiar, disappears, so to speak, from view in their *Seele*. But they notice that even without their *Gestalt*, they still know as if <u>from within</u> exactly how to behave. They also know that <u>were they observing the *Gestalt*, it would be showing them precisely what it is they are now doing independently</u>. To begin with, this only occurs momentarily. Then the *Gestalt* keeps reappearing and disappearing during rehearsals, but it is vital for this to occur <u>by itself</u>; actors should never chase off their *Gestalt*, but calmly rehearse and wait until it disappears for short periods of time <u>of its own accord</u>. This occurrence is a sign that the fourth stage is gradually approaching.

A Path – Fourth Stage

This stage arrives by itself. The actors undergo a major, important transformation, and the goal of their entire previous work has been this transformation. This fourth, last stage is the happiest moment for them. They <u>become one</u> with the *Gestalt*. Henceforth the *Gestalt* disappears from outside. It is <u>within</u> each actor. They no longer see their *Gestalt*. They no longer need to imitate it – they sense its direct effect and it uses the actor's body without any mediation. It uses everything that the actor has prepared for it by way of a 'special technique'. The *Gestalt* descends into the actor's body.

But what is it that happens to the actor? A miracle occurs. They are no longer an ordinary, everyday person. Their individuality is awakened, they experience themselves in their higher individual consciousness, and they acquire the concrete experience of a <u>split</u> in their consciousness. Just as before, sitting within their own body and following the life of the *Gestalt* <u>from outside</u>, they now follow, also <u>from outside</u>, their own physical presence, where the *Gestalt* is living and acting. Now two beings are present: on the one hand, the actor's individuality and, on the other, the imaginary *Gestalt* in the actor's body and *Seele*. This is truly the moment of <u>inspiration</u>: an imaginary *Gestalt*, a <u>geistig</u> being that they themselves have created in the world of *Gestalten* <u>inspires</u> the actor's body and *Seele*, and through this <u>inspiration</u> the actor's individuality is awakened.

This inspired imaginary being carries within it the effects of the actor's individuality. It is a being that has come about through the effect of the Idea. It is permeated with the *Seele*, with atmosphere, it is a rhythmic being and is furthermore alive with the radiation of the actor's individuality. It is itself an imaginary *Geist* and is alive with truth. Thus it inspires the actor's body and *Seele*. It is through this in-spiration that the actor's individuality is freed, and this freedom, this self-recognition (awakening) on a higher level of consciousness is for the artist a joyful, *seelisch* experience. <u>From what</u> is the artist (their individuality) <u>freed</u> in the moment of inspiration, in this creative state? They are freed from their egotism, from the influence of their small 'ego'. This comes about because in the creative moment all the forces of the actor's *Seele* are <u>deprived</u> of the small ego, the egotism. They are now led, used, guided, by the '*Geist*', the imaginary *Gestalt*. This *Gestalt* will for a time be 'the egotist', so to speak, of the actor's body and *Seele*.

Once deprived of all the *Seele* forces of the actor's small 'ego', these other *Seele* forces that are, as we have discussed previously, purified, transformed, and 'artistic matter', acquire their full power and vitality. The small 'ego' meanwhile, not being thus transformed, simply isn't active during inspiration. Now, because the newly arrived 'ego' is only an imaginary being, its 'egotism' is also imaginary and cannot pursue any earthly-personal goals. It is simply a manifestation of the artistic Idea of the actor's individual consciousness, and because of this the actor's *Seele* will be <u>purified</u> by being led and guided by this being. The body will be <u>ennobled</u>. Similarly, the actor's individuality will in its own way be purified and ennobled. This occurs because during the work, throughout all three previous stages, it has mainly been dealing with the <u>Idea</u> of the character, and now that this has been grasped and belongs to them, their *Weltanschauung* has been enriched by it. The Idea meanwhile has also acquired an individual quality, and this is an indication of the higher meaning of inspiration, of artistic creation generally, for artists personally.

Now we may pose the question: how can artists purify and ennoble themselves, if for instance they play a <u>negative</u> part? Let us recall the comparison we made previously (Second Stage) between the method for playing a character without first imagining the Idea (in this case of evil), and that of creating the play's Idea and character first in the world of the imagination. In the first, there is no purification of the mind, no ennobling of the body and no recognition of the emerging *Geist*. In such cases actors awaken and strengthen within themselves the negative forces in their own *Seele*. Audiences easily become gripped by such performances but experience <u>emotional stress</u>, and actors working in a naturalistic way always assert that during the performance they see nothing around them, don't notice the audience. Actors familiar with the split of consciousness, meanwhile, would never say such a thing, they see all that is around and never forget the audience; indeed being <u>with</u> them is something actors rely on for the performance.

The second method, meanwhile, also allows actors to <u>recognize</u> the negative type that they are playing and <u>demonstrate</u> this negative Idea in the form of their character. But they <u>will never themselves</u> be possessed by such a negative type, having split their consciousness and remained perfectly objective during rehearsals and the performance. If the evil is <u>recognized</u>, then it is also conquered. That is the true task of the artist, while if one is possessed by evil, it cannot be recognized and conquered. As we create on stage, the freed, enriched individuality guides the entire process, and furthermore it is able to observe its own Work as if with the eyes of the audience. One result of the performance being thus guided and inspired is that the Idea manifests itself on stage precisely as it should be seen today by contemporary audiences. The freed awoken individuality is a wise being and is able to perceive the audience's hearts. It sees what the audience needs, what they seek, and it wisely gives them that which they need. It wants to make them a gift of its unique Idea and seeks the correct, wise path leading to the audience's heart. It radiates powerful atmospheres and creates a strong and sure connection between the auditorium and the stage. And whenever the atmosphere is present, so too the possibility for the audience to replicate the artistic Idea.

But what is it that the *seelisch*-physical being that finds itself on stage experiences? It is completely given over to inspiration. It has truly become an instrument on which the individuality plays its melodies. One characteristic of this state is that actors sense that nothing can disturb them in their acting, no new *mise-en-scène* by their partners, no chance shifts in the precisely rehearsed blocking, no repositioning of the set etc. And more importantly, actors in such a state never need to repeat themselves. They are free every time, they receive new inspiration for the same part, every time they create their character afresh. No mechanization, no 'manual work' threatens them. Nothing can cause the individuality guiding the acting to stray. It is able to give expression to its Idea in diverse ways. It just needs to have a properly working instrument and it needs *seelisch* and physical truth. (Figure VI)

Afterword

This book is intended to be practical. It won't have achieved its aim if the method suggested here doesn't find a readership that seeks to implement it. This is first and foremost just an outline. There are presently many actors who long for a new path and seek this path, but practical directions are lacking. It is precisely these directions that this book attempts to provide.

To begin with there might be a small group of actors that studies this book, and it is not very important how quickly they manage to progress. To begin, this is perhaps the hardest, but also the most important thing – we must take the first step. We must start with the exercises and through them immerse ourselves in the secret depths of our artistic *Seele*, our bodies, our capacity to imagine. The correct paths will surely be found. What might such a small group of yearning, seeking actors need in order to take a second step? They need no theatre space, no scenery, no costumes – nothing. It would actually be dangerous to show one's initial experiences in the framework of a large theatre. So many powerful associations, feelings, habits and opinions are tied up with the old theatre that early, tender, young new shoots will surely suffocate in such surroundings. If one were to prepare a modest play, perhaps a few individual scenes – if these scenes were shown to a circle of spectators, this would be perfectly sufficient to begin with.

If life says 'yes' to such experiments, then the right means will come to help in the right moment. Confidence, work and goodwill, this is all that a small group of actors needs. An improvised, sketchy suggestion of scenery, as well as costumes, perhaps with no makeup – this too has its charm and power of persuasion. First everything must be provided inwardly. And anyway, what could old scenic and other theatre habits give these new explorations? Perhaps they are not at all necessary. First the inner paths must be found. Then the outer can gradually be added in the right style, in harmonious context with the inner. We mustn't forget that there are also audiences that long for and impatiently await deeper forms of theatre. These audiences and such actors won't find each other right away. We must not be in a hurry, we must work patiently.

The book will itself gather together only such souls that have this desire, who strive for a theatre built on the forces of an artistic individuality. And that is perfectly sufficient for the beginning. A true materialist, or an actor completely taken in by naturalism, will have no interest in this book. The question of the *Weltanschauung* is in practice not a complicated matter. Everything comes about of its own accord and everything is much simpler than perhaps it appears here. Every *Weltanschauung* is correct if only it doesn't wish to be comprehensive and alone. We must think materialistically about matter and spiritually about the *seelisch-geistig* forces of the world. A spiritual person who rejects matter makes just as great a mistake as the materialist who denies the *geistig* forces of the world.

We shouldn't think that this book represents any particular *Weltanschauung*. No, this book is an impartial artistic vision for the world, and the *Weltanschauung* will develop by itself in the *Seelen* of those working together. Workers in a factory during their shift think as the machines demand of them. To do differently would be impossible, otherwise there will be an accident, a catastrophe. The work will to a greater or lesser degree influence the thinking of those working, and this is so in all fields of life. Someone doing *geistig* work acquires in their thinking a quality corresponding to the *Geist* with which they are connecting to. This is a wise and fine law in life.

So a group of actors who gather around this idea of theatre should simply begin working. The noble, refined matter and ideas with which these actors approach their work will in time do the rest. All that is necessary is a real will and work.

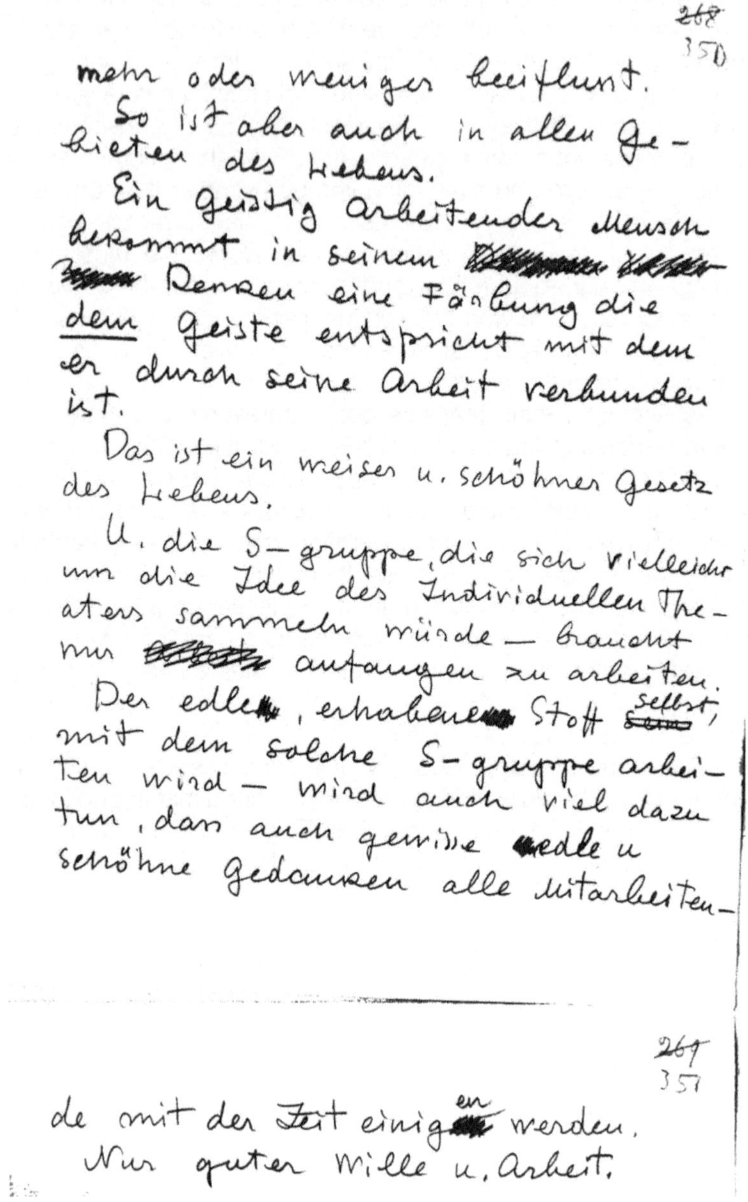

mehr oder weniger beeinflusst.
So ist aber auch in allen Gebieten des Lebens.
Ein geistig arbeitender Mensch bekommt in seinem ~~Wirken~~ ~~Willen~~ ~~Wesen~~ Denken eine Färbung die dem Geiste entspricht mit dem er durch seine Arbeit verbunden ist.

Das ist ein weises u. schöhnes Gesetz des Lebens.

U. die S-gruppe, die sich vielleicht um die Idee des Individuellen Theaters sammeln würde — braucht nur ~~~~ anfangen zu arbeiten.

Der edle, erhabene Stoff selbst, mit dem solche S-gruppe arbeiten wird — wird auch viel dazu tun, dass auch gewisse edle u schöhne Gedanken alle Mitarbeiten-

de mit der Zeit einigen werden.
Nur guter Wille u. Arbeit.

FIGURE 28 *Last page of the 'Paris Manuscript' (numbered 350 & 351).*

Reflections from the Studio

In the section of the 'Paris Manuscript' called A Path – First Stage, Chekhov talks about an Idea-carrying play naturally expanding in different directions, something probably akin to those moments when we are lucky enough to find our way into a creative flow and sense we can barely capture all that is bubbling up from we know not where and expanding in many directions. The following texts are presented in this spirit and have emerged from engaging with the 'Paris Manuscript' and allowing it resonate through a few of the kaleidoscope of experiences that Thaís Loureiro and I encountered while working with artists at our studio, Michael Chekhov Brasil. Like Chekhov's ur-text they are aimed primarily at independent-minded actors and small groups of seekers and, in a passing nod to the annex of exercises missing from document in Zurich, several offer suggestions for further practical work, as well as providing some additional commentary generally. Given the great emphasis that Chekhov lay on concentration and imagination and how much Thaís and I explored what are ultimately two sides of the same coin ourselves, it is no wonder that this duo looms large in these pages. The Reflections close with an excerpt from a Goethe/Chekhov-inspired poem that Thaís wrote about the actor's creative experience.

Readers will note that although no translation is involved here, I have been unwilling to forgo all the advantages of having already established in this book the usage of those pivotal German words *seelisch/Seele, geistig/Geist, Gestalt* and *Weltanschauung*.

La petite bergère

Several years ago my dearly beloved (sadly since departed) brother had to undergo surgery in Switzerland and I went over to help him through it. A week or so after getting out of hospital he was just about well enough to travel, which for my brother meant only one thing: we were going on a trip. I had long hoped to one day see first-hand the Isenheim Altar, Matthias Grünewald's masterpiece that today stands in the Musée Unterlinden in Colmar, so I managed to persuade him to head north and into Alsace.

A few days later, we climbed the steps into the chapel where the Grünewald stands, and after a deeply inspiring hour I emerged to discover the museum also has an extensive collection spanning other artists from Grünewald's time right up to the twentieth century. As can easily happen in small museums, I found myself being drawn into worlds very distant in time and *Weltanschauung*, and soon became intrigued by a room of nineteenth-century works by painters from the Alsace region. As I worked my way around the images I noticed that the only other visitor present was studying just one of the works, and doing so quite intensely, so when I came to that wall, rather than encroaching on her space I simply moved around with the intention of perhaps returning to 'her' picture later. However, having reached the far end I saw that she was still there, gazing intently and apparently oblivious to my presence, even as I walked back to loiter behind her, by now curious about what it was intrigued her so. From what I could make out, the painting was unremarkable enough, a figure sitting in profile.

She turned to go and, noticing me, glanced with a knowing smile, as if to say: 'You'll see'. To begin with, though, I couldn't see very much of note, just a fairly plain portrait of a young woman with a full head of long, reddish-brown hair, wearing a blue smock, and who appears to be holding a rod or staff leaning diagonally across her right shoulder. A glance at the title card on the wall beside the frame revealed her to be *La petite bergère* by Jean-Jacques Henner, so a young shepherdess, but really, nothing remarkable, surely.

It was only when I turned back from the card and locked into the gaze that I suddenly found my way into deep fascination, for although *La petite bergère* is delicately painted and depicts a physically graceful woman, it is also the portrait of an incredibly powerful will force, of an inner life of great intensity. Before long I realized that I too was becoming willingly mesmerized by the way in which every atom of her being is <u>with</u> the object of her attention. The physical calm cannot hide her great determination, and there is clearly an element of dissent concerning whatever it is that is consuming her, apparently something or someone some distance away to our left, well out of frame.

Then something shifted and I found myself becoming further intrigued by the notion that her focus might instead be on something on her mind, that she is working through in her imagination. We cannot know, but what is not in dispute is that it means a very great deal to her, for her connection is utterly alive: there is room for nothing else within her *Seele*. She is, as the oft-memed phrase has it, burning inside with an outer ease.[43] *La petite bergère* is a portrait of utter concentration and imminent action that, when it comes, will undoubtedly be unwavering, clear and consequential. Were an actor to play her, she would have to create and sustain a very powerful inner stream indeed, in order to experience and radiate out to us

FIGURE 29 *Jean-Jacques Henner.* La petite bergère, *c. 1890. Photo © Musée d'Unterlinden, Dist. RMN-Grand Palais/image Musée Unterlinden de Colmar. For a full colour reproduction of Henner's shepherdess, please visit www.bloomsburyonlineresources.com/the-paris-manuscript-the-early-draft-rediscovered.*

this perfectly still tempest of life flowing so wildly, freely, this great breathtaking *seelisch-geistig* movement, as she sat there in the blue smock costume, serenely poised, hands resting gracefully in her lap.

I am not sure how long I remained there drawn into the world of *La petite bergère*, but I do know how far I travelled, then and since, and I'm aware that this is thanks to the power of a certain type of concentration – 'a particular kind of attention', Chekhov calls it in the first lines of the 'Paris Manuscript' – and in this case a chain of sharing a powerful will force that has endured the passage of time and lives on to this day in Colmar. It arose first in Henner's young model, who was able to create and generously sustain a moment of intense, dramatic inner life,[44] then in the artist, who succeeded in finding the right activity to experience her moment so completely himself that he was able to express it on canvas. Well over a century later, this painting touched a woman and awoke in her a creative concentration that left me curious enough to also receive this gift, to become deeply involved in the work of a not particularly well-known nineteenth-century artist. Of course, we needn't revert to stories of out-of-the-way corners of French museums to find examples of the power of concentration, they abound in everyday life, from the activity of busy animals, to children at play, to a technician repairing some machinery or gadget, to a sudden encounter with something of unusual beauty: if the concentration is full-bodied and, particularly, fully *seelisch-geistig*, it is always fascinating to observe, contagious even. The central pillar of Chekhov's ideas about the 'Theatre of the Future', as presented here, is the prescient observation that for artists working in our world of advancing technology, materialism and mechanization, this attention is something we must train and master and be able to call upon and trust at will. Indeed we can, I believe, recognize this trait in so many great artists today, regardless of their background and training. For actors in particular, meanwhile, there is an additional delight in full concentration *à la petite bergère*, which is this: there is only one circumstance more divine than a perfect instant of creative concentration, and that is experiencing it while we are being observed by others.

I was put in mind of *La petite bergère*'s intensely lived centennial pause by the section of the 'Paris Manuscript' entitled *Gestalt*, where Chekhov writes [74]:

This work of observing in the world of *Gestalten* with an altered sense of space and time affects actors in a particular way: it gradually imbues them with the character's force and the ability, so to speak, to <u>radiate something whole</u>, irrespective of any theatrical resources. Even during the performer's first entrance on stage the audience must sense, through this radiating, something of the destiny of the entire part. It is not just through the make-up, costume, movement, type of speech etc. that the destiny of the character is to be understood, it must also be felt through this radiating.

If actors are able to sense their parts like this, then so will the audience, and regardless of which words are spoken, which actions performed, whether the part is large or small, audiences will sense and experience a <u>character type</u> with <u>its destiny</u> and atmosphere. Such is the actor's lofty task.

This in turn echoes something the great Russian writer Andrei Bely once wrote about Chekhov's own acting, after seeing him play Hamlet in the legendary Second Moscow Art Theatre (MAT2) production of 1924, nearly a decade before he and Boner worked on the 'Paris Manuscript' together:

> Chekhov plays from the 'pause' – other actors play from the word. Once Chekhov enters into the role he appears from the centre *silently*. In *Hamlet* he sits looking away. Before his first words are spoken the full character of Hamlet is given from beginning to the end. Everything that will develop later is contained in that first action – as in a grain of wheat. From the pause – to the word. But in this pause is the colossal strength of potential energy at a moment when all the body is like lightning. From the peak of this lightning comes an outburst of energy, and this is the word. The word is the last of all expressions. With others, the word is first. Then comes the gesture of the face or the movements of the hands or feet, which are often not fixed. With them the pause is like an exhaled breath which comes after the word – an act of passivity. The pause is like a yawn. With Chekhov the pause is an in-breathing which fills the blood with life and makes the muscles move. The gesture flies from the pause like an arrow zigzagging lightly through the air. From the gesture is born the word, as the fruit of all action.[45]

The First Condition

In Deirdre Hurst du Prey's record of eighteen preparatory classes that Chekhov gave her and Beatrice Straight in the spring of 1936, now known as the 'Lessons for Teachers', he devotes the entire first class and a full half of their next eight meetings to the development of the artist's concentration through constant training:

> For us 'concentration' has a special meaning. It is our method for contacting and merging with the creative spiritual forces. It is the door by which we can enter into the creative spiritual world. We must train ourselves in order to develop our powers of <u>conscious concentration</u>. This is done in three steps: first by exercises which help us to contact and communicate with physical things and to free their 'spirit'. These exercises commence with seeing and hearing. In the second step, we begin to be able to imagine the objects of the physical world. In this stage we are beginning to be able to do without the help of actually seeing and hearing the object. In the third step, we pass into the vast world of the <u>creative imagination</u> where we can enter at will.[46]

Not very much time had elapsed since Chekhov and Boner had been collaborating on the draft of their text, so it is no surprise to find him emphasizing the *seelisch-geistig* throughout these sessions (albeit no longer having those handy adjectives to hand). Then towards the end of that same year, on 5 October 1936, the Chekhov Theatre Studio opened at Dartington Hall. These are the very first remarks that Michael Chekhov made to his fledgling group of young actors:

> It is very important that during the lessons you must be very active at all times. Your body must be beautiful during the whole lesson. In whatever you are doing, you must feel yourself full of power, full of energy, and never allow yourself to be a bit weaker and use the chairs to help you. These things we must avoid once and forever. In our school everybody is beautiful, everybody is strong, healthy, and very active.
> That is our style, and if we try always to be like that, you will see very soon the people who belong to our kind of school and those who do not. You must have great pleasure in staying with

us. You must feel that you are doing it with great pleasure. That is a very important feeling for an artist: to do everything with great pleasure and joy. You must be gay and serious at the same time; young and clever, powerful and soft. We are going study this way in our school.

We aim to be actors and more than actors, artists. What does this mean? It means we are going to study, to learn how we can have our inspiration at our command. That is a difficult task, but we shall have a method which will make it possible, and the first condition is that we must be able to concentrate.[47]

Chekhov then led a concentration exercise, the very first practical activity at the studio. A laminated copy of these beautiful opening remarks was pinned permanently to our notice board at Michael Chekhov Brasil and read out to all our groups, and Thaís and I took seriously Chekhov's perpetual insistence on building actors' work upon the foundation of artistic concentration. Already in the 'Paris Manuscript' Chekhov is unambiguous: 'Actors must first develop this trait within themselves, because without it they cannot carry out the exercises correctly and productively. In fact, the entire creative process depends on this trait' [29]. Although in everyday usage, the word 'concentration' is commonly understood as mental, intellectual power, Chekhov is always clear and means by it our ability to 'feel for' a *Gestalt*, whether that is a physical object, an imagined image or character, a remembered sunset, a piece of music or an abstract idea; in other words, to form a *seelisch-geistig* and creative, significant and essentially <u>transformative</u> connection to both the tangible and incorporeal worlds generally, something we might then be able to express artistically. Here he walks closely in Goethe's footsteps in inviting us to experience and essentially (re)create the object being observed within ourselves. Constant emphasis on concentration as a foundation ability permeates the work developed at the Chekhov Theatre Studio; meanwhile, of the four works he wrote about acting,[48] *To the Actor* stands out as being the only text <u>not</u> to open with an exposition of artistic concentration; in fact, the book barely mentions it at all.

Now, let us not pretend that introducing into an acting class a simple concentration exercise is a perfectly straightforward matter. I well recall the first time we decided to do so and our great anxiety that at least some of the actors present might conceivably baulk at being asked to sit on the floor staring at objects in a certain way. But having found its way into our pedagogy, this practice quickly became a mainstay of our training work and popular with the artists who came to explore with us. Before long, participants couldn't attend even just a couple of hours of our introductory workshops without learning at least one concentration exercise, while our two-month training groups were required to practise concentration with objects at least once a day for the entire period.[49] Within a week or two, the difference in the breadth of their engagement and means of expression was already clear both to them and to Thaís and myself, and particularly the life of their imaginations, which were becoming unmistakably 'more profound and precise' and 'clear and absolutely concrete', as Chekhov puts it [30]. So much so, in fact, that we began to truly understand concentration and imagination as two sides of precisely the same coin.

These are the steps we would commonly lead our students through as a starting point:

- choose an object, preferably something simple, without great significance.

- sit comfortably facing it and begin to observe and describe inwardly to yourself its physical properties (colour, shape, size, the play of light and shadow, lines and curves, details and marks etc.).

- your mind may wander with associations, or you'll feel your attention waning, in which case simply renew your interest in some part of the object's physical properties, and thus sustain your connection to and growing familiarity with the object's physical aspects.

- do not become an analytical scientist, but instead begin to sense you are observing with all your senses, that the object is 'showing itself to you' and is available to you.

- notice what it is to be in the object's presence and feel that you are truly 'with' the object now.

- close your eyes and continue to describe the object's physical properties to yourself, except now you see everything in your mind's eye.

– after a while, open your eyes and reconnect with the object visually for a few moments, then stand, turn your back on the object and move about the space, but all the while remain 'with' the object in spirit. You will observe how clearly the object remains with you somehow, that you can be fully with it now, even though you no longer see it with your eyes, and even as you start to improvise a few actions or tasks or have brief exchanges with the others in the room.

– if you find the favourable inner activity, it will now feel like you are somehow being 'held' by the object, and you no longer have to do very much beyond sustaining your awareness. This is an activity quite distinct from remembering it – in fact it has if anything very little to do with mental effort or our memory, being a full-bodied *seelisch-geistig* activity. If your object has been a chair, for instance, then you will certainly have a strong image in your mind (*Geist*), but perhaps more importantly ringing within your *Seele* will be a clear intuitive sense of that object's 'chair-ness' (both the physical and its essential 'character'). This brings great freedom, and indeed there will be little danger of 'losing' the object until you choose to let it go.

It is rewarding to work with objects of different qualities and characteristics and notice the distinct inner life that each awakens within us. Once familiarity and proficiency in finding the 'right activity' of this simple but profound basic exercise has been acquired, the variations and applications are infinite, both individually and in group work. One final caution: although the exercise establishes a subjective, unique and meaningful connection to the object of observation, this relationship should never become everyday-personal, possessive or in any way precious ('my special object').

A Gift Received

Deirdre Hurst du Prey's record of the 'Lessons for Teachers' of 1936 includes many wonderful suggestions for concentration exercises, and then in Lesson XIII we come across the diagram in Figure 30.

In the accompanying text du Prey records Chekhov as saying: 'In this scheme we see the spiritual and creative as against the material and uncreative. But we must work to incorporate the creative with the uncreative ... we must "erect" our heavy, uncreative materialistic qualities, into which we must incorporate our spiritual ideas, our inspiration, and all those creative qualities that we can get from our living spirit.'[50] Clearly the diagram is derived from the sketched drawings distributed across the 'Paris Manuscript' charting the human experience of creative inspiration, and these images are in turn a simplified version of a series of beautiful colour illustrations that Chekhov produced for his Lithuanian acting group at around the same time as he and Boner were working on the German text.[51]

In the 'Paris Manuscript', Chekhov himself goes over these at each stage, but it may be enlightening for us to study them as a sequence and compare this progression to our own personal experience. First of all (Figure 31), he illustrates our ordinary, everyday abilities to move and speak – and even to imagine – as a horizontal line lying along the ground, adjacent to the material world. We may see this

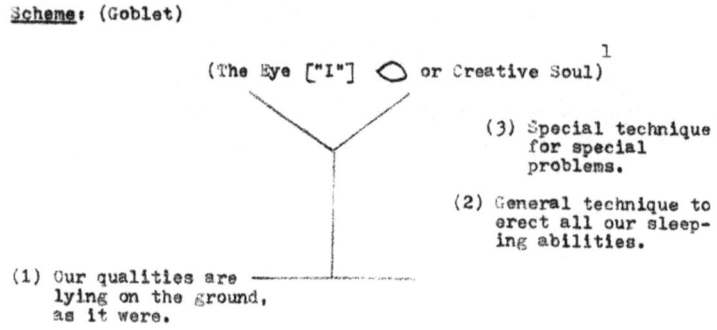

FIGURE 30 *'Goblet' diagram from du Prey's transcription of Chekhov's 19 May 1936 class, Estate of Deirdre Hurst du Prey.*

bottom line as representing the artistic qualities that lie dormant within us, our yet to be realized potential.

When we practise our craft and train, these come alive, are awoken and developed generally (the vertical line). Although we are not yet working on anything specific (say a character), we are nevertheless in a very real sense 'rising up', lifting ourselves spiritually. Through constant practice it will be possible to erect an entire cathedral of physical and *seelisch* skills, something Chekhov refers to as a general acting technique. This first drawing comes in the opening section of the manuscript, Attention [28], where he emphasizes that no general acting technique can be developed without an ability to <u>experience</u> all that we engage with from both the manifest and incorporeal worlds – in other words, to concentrate.

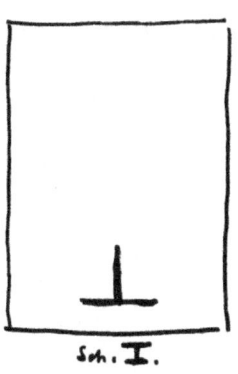

FIGURE 31 *Sketch I in the 'Paris Manuscript'*.

In the second drawing [38] (Figure 32; see also Figure 17) we again see our everyday abilities lifted up through our general acting technique, and now the world of our imagination is represented as a 'fog' all around us. This too is general and vague and Chekhov draws it high up, since that is where we experience our ideas and imagination in particular, with our immaterial life being sensed both in and around us. In workshops when we ask participants where they imagine things, many will point to their heads, which is presumably correct neurologically speaking, but <u>experientially</u> when we imagine (even something as mundane as whether to go to the pharmacy or the supermarket first), this is surely something we 'do' <u>around</u> the upper part of our presence in the space, and 'elsewhere' in a cognitive sense; we even tend to look around or up as we do so, seeking the answer 'out there'.

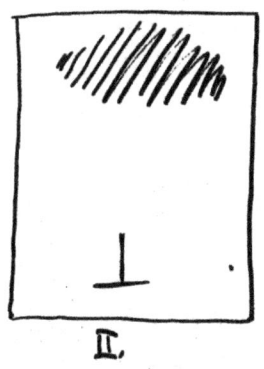

FIGURE 32 *Sketch II in the 'Paris Manuscript'*.

The images in our imaginations are fleeting and delicate but, as with the traits of the general technique, they quickly acquire form once we start to work on something specific and, as we begin to engage with it, our individuality comes into play: in the third drawing [53] this is represented as a shining light, a star that illuminates and unifies the world of the imagination and our cathedral of general skills (Figure 33).

We are all familiar with this moment, even from the simplest of exercises, when we sense that something is developing: it feels like an inner light 'arriving'. In the case of an actor engaging with a character, it is the individuality that 'finds' the *Gestalt* for us, the form of the character in the imagination. To begin with this may not be terribly clear, but just as even the faintest light is always enough to get our bearings in a dark room, here too we will invariably receive just enough to allow us to trust finding our way.

FIGURE 33 *Sketch III in the 'Paris Manuscript'*.

The fourth image in this sequence of illustrations is sadly missing. In the original text, the last line of the section A Path – Second Stage carries an instruction for Boner – 'You can stick Diagram IV here' – and the accompanying description reads: 'A hazy, unformed <u>whole</u> will be brought together in the actors' individuality and through active inner work they find certain forms'. Although absent from the surviving manuscript, we may picture a progression from the previous drawing with some form of concrete character emerging and shaping us.

The fifth drawing comes in A Path – Third Stage [101] (Figure 34; see also Figure 26) where Chekhov describes how, as the actor starts to be able to embody the character from the increasingly clear experience of the *Gestalt* in the imagination,

FIGURE 34 *Sketch V in the 'Paris Manuscript'*.

what is being developed is actually nothing other than an entire acting technique specifically for this character. He calls this a 'special technique' and uses the image of a cup forming (or goblet, as du Prey recorded later) as we reach upwards to be shaped further, become spirit and receive the character moving down from the actor's *seelisch-geistig* world and become manifest through us, an exchange whereby we bring the specific creative spirit into our physical body and embody it using our 'intangible means of expression'.[52]

In the final illustration, right at the end of A Path – Fourth Stage [107], the actor achieves a state of complete inspiration, has been utterly transformed inwardly and outwardly, is being constantly 'filled' to the brim by the connection to the *geistig-seelisch* world they have created in partnership with that very world – specifically and uniquely for this character (Figure 35). Any sense of technique or 'doing' recedes and now the character just is, leaving the actor perfectly free and confident.

FIGURE 35 *Sketch VI in the 'Paris Manuscript'*.

There may be a danger that we view these diagrams in some reverential way, something distant to be attained one magical day, whereas I believe all of us will have experienced everything that Chekhov is describing here in moments of intense creative connection to something. Laid out in this way they are certainly far more schematic and less fluid than our actual creative life, which is essentially a river that we must seek to keep flowing. Certainly there would be no point in seeing these as steps to be followed diligently in numerical order, a progression of 'how to', and as Chekhov writes about the four stages of A Path, they are presented to 'help actors, rather than disturb them or make them pedantic' [77].

I do, however, find this knowledge helpful as a way of getting a better sense of what our own experience of moments of inspiration will feel like, and through this recognize the flow of our creative work. I suspect we should view the progression portrayed here as a great experiential kaleidoscope that is constantly flowing, ringing, merging and filling us within, with the elements from all these beautifully sketched illustrations rising and falling simultaneously and to different degrees, as soon as we begin to work and find the right activity.

More Concrete than a Memory, More Organized than a Dream

Here is Chekhov in Ridgefield, Connecticut, on 25 January 1940, conducting a wonderful variation on a concentration exercise during a class devoted entirely to imagination and concentration, and easily adapted and practised today:

> You must accept concentration as something to which you must aspire. You must do these exercises every day or your work will be lost. We know that rhythmical repetition does more good than violent effort today which is followed by days of doing nothing. Five minutes each day will give you more than spasmodic efforts of longer time. If you will develop your ability to concentrate, your imagination will grow as if of itself. When your imagination is strong, this ability to concentrate your attention and keep the object on which you are concentrating like a stone in your heart, that is the aim ... To be concentrated on something does not mean to be concentrated with one sense – it means to be concentrated with all our senses, all our abilities which the human being has, whether we know them or not ... It will be a miracle, and you will discover new things which you did not know existed; such qualities and depths of things. Only if we grasp the object with our whole being, with all our powers and forces which we have in our living being, will the miracle happen.
>
> Exercise: Concentrate all your abilities on the lamp – try to see it – then stretch your hand and try to touch it, although you cannot because of the distance, but get the feeling that you are touching it. Certain powers must be awakened in us if we see and touch this distant thing with our whole being. Then shut your eyes and touch it without seeing. Try to increase this feeling of being more free, and not in your bodies, as it were. Try to grasp the lamp and possess it with your whole being. Try to penetrate into it, and saturate the lamp with your whole being, and become almost one with it. Be so strongly merged with the lamp that you feel its weight. Try to penetrate the glass and guess the quality of the lamp, being in it – how hard, how breakable, how elastic – all these qualities must be yours. Now you will feel that you are

streaming to the lamp, that you are flowing to it. You can get it with your hearts, your hands, your soul, your whole being has the lamp. Then you will feel that you are creating the lamp at this moment – at this moment it would not exist without you because you are creating it. Now, being so much with the lamp, try to make the gesture of passive acceptance. What will come of this? The lamp will speak to you – the object will speak to you about its qualities, if you will exercise sufficiently. These qualities will arise before you like a conscious dream – more concrete than a memory and more organized than a dream.[53]

Like the four stages of the creative process, these different elements and steps for our concentration have noble origins, as we shall now see.

Goethe's Method for Observing Natural Phenomena

Recognizing the tendency of the dry, rational intellect to increasingly prevail in the scientific practice of his own times, the philosopher, scientist and literary giant Johann Wolfgang von Goethe developed his own intuitive – but nevertheless empirical – way of studying the natural world. He called this approach *zarte Empirie*, usually translated as 'delicate empiricism', which involves using our sensory and imaginative nature as a legitimate scientific tool. Not only are Chekhov's concentration exercises derived from this method, but experiencing both the physical and immaterial world around us in this way may be seen as the first element in any creative process, for:

> To create is to express that which we have within us. Every authentic creative effort is an inner one. So we must nourish our feelings, something which we do with the help of elements from the outer world. This is where the work comes in by which the artist gradually incorporates, assimilates the outer world, until the object being drawn has become a part of himself, until he has it in him and can project it onto the canvas as his own creation.[54]

This is the French painter Henri Matisse speaking in 1953, describing a universal dynamic that Jean-Jacques Henner certainly tapped into when he painted *La petite bergère*. Goethe's method develops precisely this dynamic and comprises four steps that can be readily practised and trained by anyone. All that is needed is an object of study, which for Goethe was often a plant:

1) Exact sensorial perception (*Exakte sinnliche Wahrnehmung*)

The first step is to suspend all personal judgement and our everyday evaluation, for instance whether we like or dislike the plant, what we already know about it, its name or classification, any habitual associations and memories, and so forth. We attempt to get beyond all such considerations so that we may begin to observe simply the phenomenon as it is.

Then we take time to carefully observe all the physical properties such as form, line, colour, shadow and the play of light, and as we proceed we take care to remain inwardly active and lively in our perception. Drawing the plant/object is also recommended here, in order to truly grasp its physical nature.

2) Exact sensorial imagination (*Exakte sinnliche Phantasie*)

We now introduce the element of time and recognize that all plants are part of an ongoing metamorphosis. We picture how the plant arrived at its present state (as both a whole and each individual element, its leaves, stem, buds and flowers and so forth), which is where we begin to use the imagination as a practical scientific tool. We may also get a sense of external factors, the environment, that have contributed to this present state, as well as go beyond the present to observe how the plant will continue to grow and develop in the future. In this second stage, we are able see the plant as a momentary expression of the process of its own transformation, as it moves from the past and into the future.

3) Beholding and inspiration (*Schauen und Inspiration*)

Stage three consists of a shift from the very active engagement of the first two practices, to something similar to receiving. For now we hold back and simply encounter the phenomenon with an open mind and allow it to express itself, almost as if it could speak to us. This will feel more like listening, as we open up and make ourselves available, offering the plant the capacity to express itself through us. Here we may perceive some intentionality expressed by this life form, its qualities, its 'gesture', and we simply try to step outside what has gone before and make space for the plant to be articulate in its own way through our attention.

4) The power to judge in beholding; pure phenomenon
    (*Anschauende Urteilskraft und reines Phänomen*)

At the start of A Path – Fourth Stage [105] Chekhov writes 'This stage arrives by itself', and similarly what comes next here is in practice a natural consequence of the third stage, rather than a fourth focus as such; in other words, it emerges from and grows out of the previous step. But we do need to be aware that it is coming alive within us. In English this final stage is sometimes referred to simply as 'Being one with the object'. Here we return to an activity somewhat reminiscent of our initial encounter with the phenomenon, except now we can be purely intuitive, rather than exact. We might say that the first stage involved Perception (of the form), the second Imagination (of the metamorphosis), and the third, Inspiration, allowing us to receive the essence. Now the

Intuition comes into play to both combine and go beyond the first three experiences so that we come to a deeper knowledge of the plant, something Goethe called the ur-phenomenon, or archetypal form. Ultimately, an exchange of consciousness will occur, allowing for a unity between subject and object, and we may sense that we are observing 'the plant within ourselves' just as much as the physical external phenomenon.

There is of course a direct correlation between this process and the four stages of a creative journey described by Chekhov in A Path [77–107], and this fourth stage is precisely the experience described by Matisse in the quote above. Goethe himself put it thus:

> We know ourselves only to the extent that we know the world; our awareness of it is the awareness of the world within ourselves. <u>Every new object, well contemplated, forms a new organ within us.</u>[55] [Our emphasis.]

Such *seelisch-geistig* journeys can quickly start to sound far more complicated than they are when described like this, rather than experienced. However, this work is all perfectly accessible once we actually move into practice, it is a simply a matter of discovering it for ourselves and making it our own.

Seelische Geste

One of the benefits to emerge from studying the 'Paris Manuscript' that I am particularly grateful for is the light this ur-text has shone on Chekhov's frequent use of the terms 'psychology' and 'psychological' in the later work, once he began leading classes at Dartington Hall and working on English texts with du Prey and others. This is something that has already been touched upon in the Introduction when we discussed a certain lacuna in English for ways of referring to the incorporeal, spiritual portion of our human experience, at least compared to the German language. Although ultimately a word is just a word and what really counts for artists will always be our experience and the practice itself, the constant references to our psychology do seem somewhat distracting. Of course, Chekhov's best-known exercise – Psychological Gesture – contains precisely this term, and indeed, during our years teaching together at Michael Chekhov Brasil, Thaís Loureiro and I did wonder time and again about this designation as a way of describing that particular activity, not least because we found many actors new to the work initially imagine it – perfectly reasonably, as it happens – as having something to do with a form of physical gesture that reveals the character's general psychology or current mental state (a habit, say, or fidgeting etc.).[56]

Even once one does become familiar with the true nature of Psychological Gesture, intuitive doubts or distractions may linger, given our natural instinct whenever we hear the word 'psychological' to veer head/mind-wards, rather than towards the experience of the full body, much less the lower body and its will centre, fundamental elements in the imaginative *seelisch* connection that Psychological Gesture requires, something capable of awakening within us and sustaining an overflowing creative, archetypal synthesis. Again, once we have successfully embarked on the journey of the innumerable possibilities that make up this rich means of expression, the name we give it will matter little, but as someone fascinated by language and translation who has now spent two years getting to know the 'Paris Manuscript' from various angles (reader, copyist, editor, translator), and followed this period in which gesture was emerging for Chekhov as an image for our inner experience, it has become inconceivable to me that had he continued working with Boner in German, the name chosen for these exercises would have been 'Psychologische Geste'. The terms 'psychologie' and 'psychologisch' are hardly ever used in the entire 351 pages of the manuscript, and in one instance this is actually to make an adverse point about the cold, dry intellect inferred from both the word's prefix 'psycho', and its suffix 'logical' [64].⁵⁷ Certainly 'psychological' is never used here in the same way as later on in so many English texts, to mean our inner life and incorporeal *seelisch-geistig* world, while, as you will have noted, Chekhov uses the pair of German terms in precisely this sense incessantly throughout the 'Paris Manuscript'. The vast majority of these are *seelisch/Seele*, in other words the diametric opposite of the mind-centric 'psychological' of the English (as discussed in the Introduction to this book, here Chekhov is able to differentiate between the inner life of our mind and imagination, and that of our torso, limbs and lower body).⁵⁸

Further clues about Chekhov's use of language and his precise understanding can be found in what may be seen as a transition period that began following the 1935 US tour, as he gradually started moving from Russian and German into a new idiom for him, English. A few weeks after the opening performances at the Majestic Theatre in New York in February, Beatrice Straight and Deirdre Hurst (not yet du Prey) attended three private introductory classes given by Chekhov, which were the first sessions transcribed by the latter in shorthand notes. These are unique among her vast archive of class and lecture transcriptions in that Chekhov had as yet no English, so spoke in Russian throughout, via an interpreter, Tamara Daykarhanova, a former colleague from the Moscow Art Theatre who had moved to the United States in the 1920s (Beatrice Straight had been attending Daykarhanova's classes, and incidentally, it was at her acting school on West 56th Street that any American actors interested in joining the Chekhov Theatre Studio at Dartington Hall would later apply; see Figure 36).⁵⁹

Now, the striking point regarding our present exploration of language can be found in Daykarhanova's interpretation of what Chekhov is saying in Russian, since she frequently gives us the English word 'soul', and adopts expressions like 'body life':

> You have a soul and you have a body. Your soul can have imagination, and your body can embody your imagination. The creative work is to bring the imagination to the body life.⁶⁰

And:

The soul of the actor has to have faith that the body will always be subordinated to the soul ... If the soul is in doubt, nothing will come out of the body, even if it is trained. If the soul is perfectly sure and certain that the body will do everything, then the body will express.[61]

This was only a few months after Chekhov and Boner had been working on their German book, and the echoes here of the word *Seele* and its precise usage throughout the 'Paris Manuscript' are surely unmistakable. The next recorded texts that we have are a September 1935 lecture in New York and the 'Lessons for Teachers' the following spring, during the run-up to the opening of the studio at Dartington, and in both cases Chekhov – now speaking English – boldly refers throughout to the 'soul', 'spirit' and 'spiritual', with no mention of 'psychology' and 'psychological'.[62] It is only once he moves further into the English language that these terms begin to appear more frequently, and with this particular meaning.[63]

FIGURE 36 Theatre Arts Monthly, January 1937 (inside cover). Michael Chekhov Brasil archive.

I have therefore become increasingly fascinated during my work on this book by the notion that had Chekhov remained in mainland Europe developing all this work with Boner, the most famous of his many rich contributions to the development of the actor's craft would in all likelihood have been introduced to the world as *Seelische Geste* (or perhaps *Gebärde*, another German word meaning gesture often used by Chekhov). In fact, in the 'Paris Manuscript' he comes within a hair's breadth of coining precisely this term. This is still a couple of years before the first recorded reference to Psychological

Gesture as such, but our practice of creating a complete physical movement to awaken our inner life is already described perfectly:

> The body's artistic habit of self-contained, complete gestures will work on the actor's *Seele*, thereby helping find inner *seelisch* forms as self-contained, complete **gestures** ... [33] [Our emphasis.]

And key here of course is his observation that these gestures work 'on the actor's *Seele*', rather than the *Geist* or mind.

In the late 1970s Georgette Boner produced her own German translation of the seminal 1953 publication *To the Actor*,[64] and it turns out she too may have wondered about the congruity of the frequent references to things psychological. Boner doesn't of course veer from giving her German readers the term 'Psychologische Geste', but it is the only instance in which she translates the word 'psychological' literally. Otherwise she either creatively sidesteps it, or gives interpretative translations such as 'Innenleben' (inner life), 'psyche' and, surprise, surprise...*seelisch*. Truly surprising, though, is that Boner goes well beyond her role of translator and uses considerable artistic licence to actually sneak in a couple of references to things *seelisch* of her own. In chapter 5 (on Psychological Gesture) she goes so far as to insert an entire paragraph that is not in the original: after introducing a quality of movement (caution) to emphasize that our physical movements must be able to awaken inner feelings, she writes: 'Through the power of imagination the suggested quality brings a *seelisch* content to the purely mechanical movement ... The effect of the *seelisch*-coloured and enriched gesture awakens in us corresponding sensations, which in turn create the corresponding feelings.'[65] Presumably as she worked on Chekhov's English text Boner felt the need – and was bold enough – to clarify this for German readers.

Of course, this whole discussion is purely academic, both in the sense of offering up critical speculation of what might have been had history turned out differently (the comparative merits of which others may judge), and because it naturally won't have any impact on the fact that the term 'Psychological Gesture' has long been ingrained in the language of theatre craft (as has, for that matter, 'Psychologische Geste'). Nevertheless, these reflections do I believe go well beyond a simple question of semantics, and may therefore help artists investigate further what the world of inner gesture means to them. While it is of course true that one of the elements that we wish to transform in exploring this exercise is our state of mind and the psychology, our own experience at the studio has been that this is not something that need overly concern us, since a transformed psychology is neither the means nor even the pre-eminent end of Psychological Gesture, but a happy and indeed natural consequence, just like the changes that occur in the breath, our inner tempo and outer movements, the voice and much else besides. One might say that Chekhov's exercise is far more *seelisch*-physical in essence (and once fully alive within, predominantly *seelisch*), than anything commonly understood by the word 'psychological'.

I confess that should I ever find myself teaching in German someday, it'll now be extremely hard to resist following in Boner's footsteps and 'sneaking in' the odd exploration of the alternative expression *seelische Geste*.

A Play Going on in My Head

Nowhere is the strangeness to contemporary sensibilities of parts of Chekhov's legacy in greater evidence than the section that takes up much of the second half of the 'Paris Manuscript' – the four sections of A Path – a perhaps somewhat tentative sketch describing the stages of a rehearsal process, all the while referring back to and bringing in elements that have been discussed in previous sections. Readers familiar with the 1991 publication *On the Technique of Acting*[66] will recognize this as being an ur-draft of the final chapter of that book, but taken at face value this rehearsal path certainly sounds particularly 'utopian'; as in, woefully impractical. Chekhov appears to suggest embarking on an alarmingly slow progression, including the notion that the actors and director should not only delay the distribution of parts beyond what we would generally consider feasible (and even desirable),[67] but create the characters and prepare pretty much the entire play in their minds, before even once getting up and acting anything out.

Read today from a practical point of view, these steps may well seem counter-intuitive in the extreme and, apart from anything else, would require delegating much more of the work than we will likely feel comfortable with to some incorporeal world of the imagination, with its fleeting *Gestalten* and atmospheres and rhythms. Although neither I nor indeed Chekhov himself would recommend using this early draft scheme as a blueprint ('what is being described here are simply a few laws of creation, a certain hygiene of creation, but it must all be taken very freely and used individually in practice' [86], and 'This is first and foremost just an outline.' [108]), I do believe that he was on to something here, and that all great artists of the past and present have figured out some version of this 'hygiene of creation', in the sense of allowing the imagination to be an equal partner in order to secure freedom as artists. So even if all that we take in practical terms from what Chekhov sets out here – and with a great deal of insight along the way – is a reminder that as artists we all need to create clear strategies for ensuring we are able to trust the 'concrete' world of the imagination, I do believe this Path needs to be taken seriously.

Here is playwright Edward Albee speaking in 1995 about his creative process:

I have the awareness that there is a play going on in my head, something clicks and says: 'Edward, there's a play that you're thinking about.' I start getting a very hazy sense of who the characters are. Everything is very much out of focus, in a heavy mist, and some sense of why they're all together. I keep the play in my head, and think about these things, and let it come back into focus for a long time, six months, four years sometimes. Finally it starts really coming into focus and I have some sense of who the characters are, I have some sense of what they want to do, what they don't want to do, at least why they're there and why I plan to make a play of them.

I write nothing down. I've learned that writing something down gets it completely out of my head, and I lose contact with them. So no, I don't write anything down, I make no notes, no *précis*, nothing. So I will take my characters and improvise with them for an hour or so, and if I know them very well, they can be in any scene I want to put them in, and I can trust them to be in my play.

And then I start writing. When I start writing something down, I have no idea what the first three lines of dialogue are going to be. I have some vague sense of the destination. I have not made outlines of what happens in Act I, what happens in Act II, or any of that stuff. I sort of filter it from what I have decided in my head, guiding it with my craft onto the page. That's as close as I can describe it. It's a kind of translation. From the unconscious, to the conscious, to the page.[68]

The parallels here with Chekhov's rehearsal process are surely clear (see for instance [87–8]), although again, no one would adopt Albee's personal experience of playwriting as a template; it simply sounds too chaotic and random. But he has certainly learned to trust the world of his imagination to a greater extent even than his powers of reason, and knows that in doing so his *Gestalten* will take on a life of their own far richer than anything he could think up 'by himself', it is just a matter of patiently reaching up and allowing them to come down to meet his creative consciousness. We are all familiar with this world of independent *Gestalten* from our dreaming, and Chekhov writes that 'the dreams of humankind have the style of human creation.' [87], as well as making the beautiful observation that it is in the early stages of creating a new work that 'the creative forces are gathered that are necessary for the work that lies head ... in which the director and actors breathe in the *seelisch* air.' [88].

Here is a similar account, this time concerning a musician, the American troubadour Tom Waits, as narrated by the author Elizabeth Gilbert:

> He said: 'Every single song has its own individual character and you can't treat each song the same way, because it wants to be treated differently and there are songs that are like scared birds that you have to sneak up on over the course of months in the woods ... songs that you have to bully and songs that are like dreams, songs that don't want to exist, and you have to let them go, and you have to let them not haunt you — which is another way to not become insane as an artist.'
>
> He was driving down the freeway one day in Los Angeles, and he heard a little tiny trace of a beautiful melody, and he panicked because he didn't have his waterproof paper, and he didn't have his tape recorder, and he didn't have a pen, he didn't have a pencil — he had no way to get it. And he thought: 'How am I going to catch this song?' He started to have all that old panic and anxiety that artists have, feeling like you're going to miss something, and then he just slowed down and he looked up at the sky and said: 'Excuse me, can't you see I'm driving? If you're serious about wanting to exist, come back and see me in the studio. I spend six hours a day there, you know where to find me, at my piano. Otherwise, go bother Leonard Cohen.'[69]

It is no great task to come across a host of similar accounts by and about artists from all walks of life, talking in precisely the terms that Chekhov adopts to describe the imagination as an essentially independent creative collaborator, something that as we work must be called upon far more than our everyday worldly sensibilities, and certainly more than our intellect, or than the tangible elements of the physical world. Here is another account, this time by Argentinian author Jorge Luís Borges:

> Before I begin, I generally have my first sentence more or less ready. And I always know what the last sentence should be. Then when I'm working on it, things are being revealed to me, as if the story were already there, I merely have to glimpse it, to uncover it even, like that famous story of the sculptor Rossetti where the

statue lay stored in the marble, he merely had to chip away what wasn't needed. I feel that way. I feel that stories and poems are already there.[70]

It is not only artists that have found the truth and value of such enigmas. Here are two quotes from authors who, despite being from radically disparate walks of life, appeal to very similar imagery to describe their experience of the creative process:

> The best analogy I've been able to find for that intense feeling of the creative moment is sailing a round-bottomed boat in strong wind. Normally, the hull stays down in the water, with the frictional drag greatly limiting the speed of the boat. But in high wind, every once in a while the hull lifts out of the water, and the drag goes instantly to near zero. It feels like a great hand has suddenly grabbed hold and flung you across the surface like a skimming stone. It's called planing.[71]

> Our free will can pause or hinder the course of inspiration, and when the favourable wind of divine grace fills the sails of our spirit, we are free to refuse our consent and thereby hinder the effect of the wind's favour; but when our spirit sails along and navigates favourably, it is not we who cause the wind of inspiration to blow, nor we who fill our sails, nor we who give motion to the ship of our heart, we merely receive the wind from heaven, consent to its motion and allow the ship to sail on it, without the hindrance of our resistance.[72]

The first of these sailing analogies is from a 2003 paper by American physicist Alan Lightman and the second by St François de Sales writing in the early seventeenth century.

Consider for a moment the great actors whose work you have witnessed and who have moved and inspired you. I believe you will find them to be all 'chekhovian', though not in the sense of having studied Michael Chekhov's work nor even of having heard of him,[73] but should they be persuaded to talk about how they go about creating character, or like to prepare or rehearse (most artists wisely play their cards close to their chests regarding their creative life), they will I am sure sound to some degree like Albee, Waits, Lightman, de Sales and so many others, with a personal 'system' they have come to rely on that will sound strange and perhaps even outlandish to others, but which will nevertheless be universal.

In the section on Artistic Individuality Chekhov writes [55]:

> Great individuals and artists in all eras have always striven for a <u>single</u> all-encompassing *Weltanschauung*, and hence have all been quite different. Conversely, the smaller, lower nature of individuals and artists always strives for <u>different</u> opinions, yet these always remain <u>alike</u>.[74]

And in the section on Imagination [38]:

> It is destructive and paralysing for an artist to think they are the <u>lone</u> creator in the sphere of the imagination. This thought causes the *Seele* to close in on itself and puts too much of a demand on the artist, while the world of the imagination also closes on itself and will offer them no gifts. The result is that in a certain (and subtle) sense they end up falling into a type of <u>artistic egotism and arrogance</u>. This shuts off inspiration from the actor's *Seele*. In order to have ideas, inspiration, talent, we must carry in our *Seele* the natural and self-evident feeling that there is an objective world that really can <u>give</u> actors something, and that it <u>comes in</u> to us: 'in-spiration' in the truest sense of the word.

This brings us back to Chekhov's prescient observations concerning the growing materialism and mechanization, which he realized would require actors and artists of the future to compensate for the increasing bewilderment of the *Seele*'s everyday sensibilities, through a *Geist* made concrete – in other words, a creative universe we can learn to have at our command, that we can trust to support us and give us just as much confidence as the ground beneath us that we take for granted.

Until we have joined so many great artists of the present-day 'future' foreseen by Chekhov in the discovery our own individual version of this dynamic, until we learn to trust such paths, embarking on them will seem incredibly counter-intuitive. But if we succeed, then certainly 'the lawfulness and truth of the imagination will prevail' [40] – and conversely, we should ever be wary of creative paths that are in no sense mysterious or perhaps even a little eccentric, at least to our left brain.

Course Made Good

The times that Chekhov lived in were extremely turbulent, as are today's for so many around the world. Artists face a fresh set of challenges in this our twenty-first century post-digital internet age – our 'post-truth' world, no less – and notwithstanding all the material progress that has been made since Chekhov's time, there is so much that appears to have gone not just in the wrong direction, but been essentially derailed or simply lost. So it can be tempting for us to intuitively look back at elements of past decades with a certain envy and, as we face our present, feel like the local who, having been asked by a traveller for directions, after much thought replies: 'Well, to be honest, I wouldn't start from here.'

Given the difficulties facing anyone working in the arts today, but especially young people starting out in an environment where so much dry, intellectual thinking dominates and has long been normalized, we may indeed be forgiven for wishing we were starting elsewhere. Although highly critical of naturalism in the arts, which he saw as an innate consequence of the technological progress and mechanization of society, Chekhov did recognize an opportunity for actors of the future that I believe to be relevant still today, for although there can be no underestimating the dangers of the dominance of a dry, inartistic intellect and all that 'naturalism has bequeathed the future' [67], he did nevertheless perceive a viable path in embracing both universes, the material and the *seelisch-geistig* made concrete, to form an 'art of the free individuality' [65–8].[75]

Again, when we write about such things, the mind may immediately get busy and puzzled and judgemental, but our experience in the studio is that while certainly complex, this world of creation is not so difficult to tap into in practice, not so very complicated (it is said French composer Maurice Ravel had a motto guiding his creative life: 'complexe mais pas compliqué'). It is a question of our will and of feeling our way along the right path, something lying well beyond the confines of this or that technique label.

However, the challenges themselves can certainly be both complex and complicated: how to proceed amid the careening advance of materialism and mechanization, if we are to preserve our artistic integrity? As Idries Shah's quote in the Introduction to this book points out, the perils of working within extrinsically established structures are real and often restrictive – everything from our long outdated education system, to the invasion of digital technology, to the value society affords the arts generally, even, as we have seen, to the confines of our language. Unlike periods such as the military dictatorship ruling Brazil from the 1960s to the 1980s, or that of Chekhov's homeland and the East European states occupied by the Soviet Union for much of the twentieth century, where artists and dissidents generally faced a brutally tangible source of oppression, and where maintaining creative freedom and integrity could be a matter of life and death, the greater danger for many of us now may well lie in the imperceptible normalization of a dominant overly materialistic *Weltanschauung* and the consequent dulling, reduction and even mistrust of the imagination and our immaterial life. In the 'Paris Manuscript' Chekhov shares his fears of a general debasement, and many since have had similar insights, among them the American author Ursula Le Guin:

> In America the imagination is generally looked on as something that might be useful when the TV is out of order. Poetry and plays have no relation to practical politics. Novels are for students, housewives, and other people who don't work. Fantasy is for children and primitive peoples. Literacy is so you can read the operating instructions. I think the imagination is the single most useful tool mankind possesses. It beats the opposable thumb. I can imagine living without my thumbs, but not without my imagination.
>
> I hear voices agreeing with me. 'Yes, yes!' they cry. 'The creative imagination is a tremendous plus in business! We value creativity, we reward it!' In the marketplace, the word creativity has come to mean the generation of ideas applicable to practical strategies to make larger profits. This reduction has gone on so long that the word creative can hardly be degraded further. I don't use it any more, yielding it to capitalists and academics to abuse as they like. But they can't have imagination.
>
> Imagination is not a means of making money. It has no place in the vocabulary of profit-making. It is not a weapon, though all weapons originate from it, and their use, or non-use, depends on

it, as with all tools and their uses. The imagination is an essential tool of the mind, a fundamental way of thinking, an indispensable means of becoming and remaining human.[76]

Something that can be clearly inferred from what Chekhov was beginning to explore in the 'Paris Manuscript', and which he was still talking about late in life, is the need to adjust the angle of attack of our creative work in order not only to compensate for all the 'noise', conditioning and dominance of the materialism in our times, but to sustain our ability to concentrate and imagine in the fullest sense, even as we inevitably engage with the breakneck advance of science and technology and intellectual supremacy.

Perhaps another sailing analogy may be helpful to illustrate this, the concept of 'course steered' and 'course made good' as shown in Figure 37. Initially the boat may calmly steer its course, but if, as in the second instance, it encounters a current, in other words, the entire mass of water is in tidal movement, the effect will be to cause a discrepancy between the course steered and what sailors call the 'course made good': the actual movement over ground. In other words, the sailor's intended navigation will be frustrated unless, as shown in the third picture, a course is set that compensates for the prevailing currents and enables us to recover our original intention.

The two decisive points here are firstly, that although the current may be a strong one, it is generally imperceptible to the sailor in the boat. Everything will feel perfectly normal and we will go off course unwittingly unless we have a 'higher' awareness and, ideally, previous experience to develop a sixth sense for these currents. As Chekhov warns: '[If we follow our path] unconsciously, a great

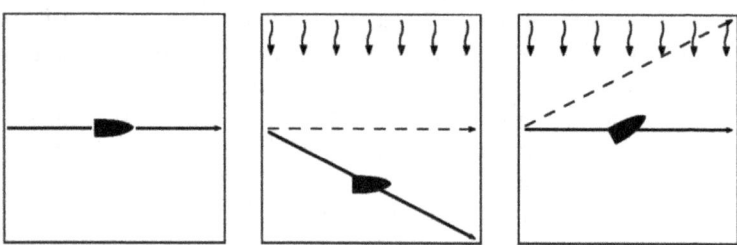

FIGURE 37 *Course steered vs. course made good. Illustration by Beatrice Moss. Michael Chekhov Brasil archive.*

danger looms: even with the best will in the world we shall be tossed back and forth artlessly and passively on the waves driving human development.' [53]. Secondly, even when we do have this awareness and set the correct course in order to 'make good', it will nevertheless always on some level <u>feel strange</u> and counter-intuitive, as if the boat were going in a direction different from the desired destination.

Although this simple nautical metaphor may not bear too much scrutiny, it does illustrate something of what Chekhov is conveying about how important it is that artists learn to trust our *seelisch-geistig* investigations and practices, despite the tide of materialism and mechanization that is now so vast that it feels perfectly normal, its effects on us being largely imperceptible. If we just set out to create art intuitively with what feels fairly natural in our *Zeitgeist*, we will inevitably end up drifting towards intellect-driven and conceptual shores: 'All well-meaning wishes for the renewal of the theatre will be futile if actors do not renew themselves. The actor is the lead part in theatre and we alone can bring life to these new paths and make them concrete.' [67].

Thinking Feeling Willing

Over the years, the many working actors attending the studio have shared a challenge about which Chekhov is lucid and indeed prescient in his early text: how incredibly difficult it can be as we move through the practicalities of theatre and film making, to stay 'grounded' in the immaterial, spiritual world of our creative life, and, as has already been discussed, all great artists will create their own ways and means, great and small, of maintaining this connection as they manage the not-always-complementary practical and creative needs and expectations. The 'Paris Manuscript' encourages us a great deal to actively develop such reflections and experiments, and particularly to seek a greater awareness of where we are 'starting from' in each and every moment.

An important benefit of having acquired the words *seelisch* and *geistig* to differentiate between the upper and lower intangible elements of our human experience is the clear recognition of how distinct these two worlds are in nature, despite being part of our own selves. This is something Chekhov would often emphasize and explore in his later practice with students at Dartington and Ridgefield,[77] and particularly the notion that although our *Geist* does capture the vast world of our imagination, ideas and dreams, it is also home to the all-powerful intellect. In the creative act, the tendency of the ever-active intellectual part of our *Geist* will always be to persuade and convince, to constantly seek to prove that things are other, and as artists we must heed Chekhov's warning that an intellect 'that has become mechanistic in the service of human beings will influence human beings like a magic spell' [64]. The *Seele*, on the other hand, has its own instinctive way of creating, expressing and transforming, which is to play and share, and although this is far richer in artistic possibilities than the intellect's powers of persuasion, it is also easily left insecure and silenced by promises of efficiency and speed (whether external or our own). As we move about the studio or rehearsal space creating and developing our characters and exploring our plays and scripts, the mere awareness of the two very distinct approaches to artistic creation within us can already bring a considerable confidence to trust in our *seelisch* powers and the particular way the *Seele* is able to interact and engage with our imagination.

Another valuable theme that Chekhov gives us here and that can be a further source of great clarity and practical use, is the notion that our inner lives are formed by a triad of perception: our Thinking, Feeling and Willing. These we experience throughout our everyday lives, but as artists they must be developed consciously as 'three main forces of the ... art of acting, requiring a particular permeability of the body in order to manifest themselves' [32–3]. In the 'Paris Manuscript' he mentions Thinking, Feeling and Willing initially in connection with movement and gesture, then develops the idea of a corresponding triad of truth, beauty and goodness [51], and explores them in relation to our *Weltanschauung*, but they are so fundamental that they may be usefully applied horizontally as an aspect of study and exploration across all stages and elements of our creative work, including, of course, creating character.

Thinking, Feeling and Willing are all inner faculties of perception and in everyday life we are only subliminally conscious of their significance and interplay. They form a whole that is experienced by all of us both intangibly and physically in the body, and here we may recall the Venn diagram in the Introduction (Figure 15) and observe that the *Seele* part of our spiritual life is experienced more around our torso and limbs, while the *Geist* acts higher up. Generally speaking, we experience Willing around the lower body and Feeling around the midsection/chest, while Thinking, of course, occurs around the head and neck. I have deliberately chosen the word 'around' because, as Chekhov frequently indicates in various ways throughout the 'Paris Manuscript', our experience of these elements is never confined to our physical contours.

This topic is infinitely more complex than we will be able to discuss here, and if you pay attention, you may even find all sorts of further thinking-feeling-willing connections around the body, for instance in the way we move. Eurythmy teaches us the beautiful movement practice of 'threefold walking', in which the raising of the heel is found to be associated to the Will, the carrying forward of the foot to Thinking, and the placing of the toes and ball of the foot to Feeling.[78] Working with actors at the studio we have found this trio of senses to be a very powerful path for awakening perceptions that gradually lead to a greater trust of the creative self over the dry intellect. For instance, artists can greatly benefit from a recognition as threefold in nature both our happy moments of inspiration, and the negative forces that frequently toss us back and forth.

Firstly let us take those fortunate times when we are 'planing', as Alan Lightman has it, and that Chekhov describes in A Path – Fourth Stage. What we experience in inspiration is surely the confidence to give ourselves over to the free flow of our Imagination (our Thinking or *geistig* world), Intuition and Impulses (the Feeling and Willing of our *seelisch* experience, respectively), with all three suddenly unhampered by everyday habits, inhibitions and distractions (see Figure 38). Even more important, though, is an awareness of and indeed familiarity with the negative forces that invariably work on us, and to avoid the common strategies of simply pretending they're not there and hoping for the best, or attempting to overcome them with brute force (usually some form of great physical and/or psychological exertion), or by appealing to a general or vague positivity. Conscious awareness of any negative forces opens up the possibility to respond clearly and with ease, and just like our inspiration, the frustrating times that all actors experience – in situations ranging from workshop sessions right

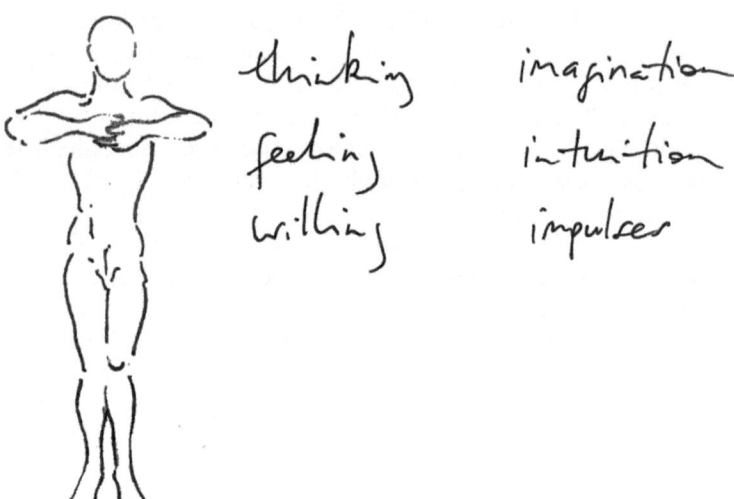

FIGURE 38 *Threefold nature of inspiration. Figure illustration: Estate Georgette Boner archives.*

through to rehearsals and moments on stage – may also be seen as threefold in nature.

The dominant negative force acting on our Thinking world is Doubt, which drags us up into a cycle of insecurity, while that which afflicts the Feeling centre and gets in the way of our creative work in that sphere is Anger. The Willing centre will in turn become racked by Fear, causing us to freeze by holding back and muting our impulses. These three negative forces invariably fuel each other in a great vicious cycle that I'm sure sounds all too familiar. Again, mere knowledge and awareness of this chain of negative forces can be truly transformative, a theme Chekhov returns to again and again, from the 'Paris Manuscript' ('If the evil is recognized, then it is also conquered.' [106–7]) to the lectures he gave decades later, at the very end of his life:

> Everyone knows by personal experience that there are two currents working within us, two powers, one good, positive, creative, helping, and another negative, hampering, destroying. Now, if we do not know about these positive, creative powers, they become weak, always weaker, their influence upon us becomes almost unnoticeable, and perhaps might disappear altogether if we never pay attention to them. Quite the opposite, if we do not know anything about the destructive, bad and hampering powers working within us, they grow, they develop, their influence upon our creative work becomes stronger and stronger. And vice versa: if we do know about our positive powers, they begin to grow and help us in our creative work.[79]

So what are the trio of positive forces that may offer a path to countering these all too familiar hindrances of Doubt, Anger and Fear? In the case of our Thinking centre, the Doubt may be countered by inviting in an intuitive sense of Clarity, while the two negative forces of the *Seele*, Anger and Fear (Feeling and Willing centres), will be soon be left powerless if we usher in Love and Courage, respectively (see Figure 39).

It is important to realize that what we are discussing is not the same as encountering solutions to specific problems in our work, but rather an intuitive beckoning of light into the darkness, something intangible but also absolutely specific that we are able to lean into. Although presented here in a somewhat schematic way, it

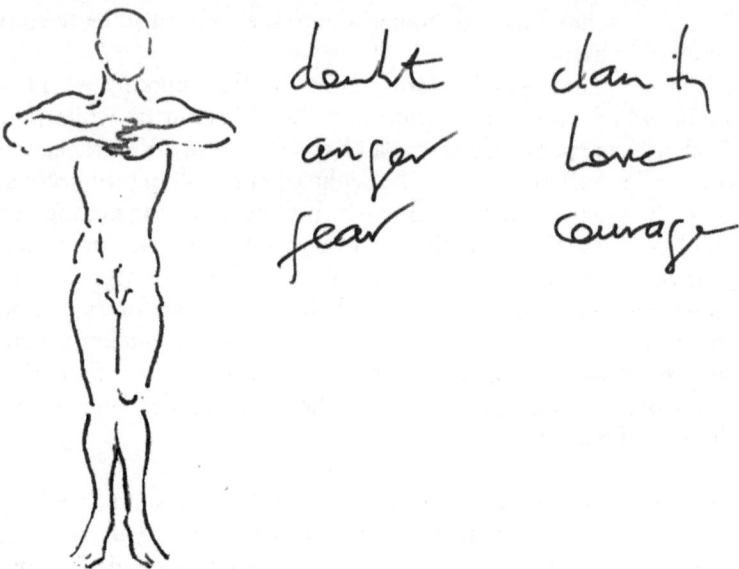

FIGURE 39 *Threefold negative and positive forces. Figure illustration: Estate Georgette Boner archives.*

is to be hoped that these further aspects of our cognitive, immaterial world may be experimented with and their practical use found to be at our disposal always, especially whenever we recognize those negative forces looming and need to recover confidence in the ever reliable support of the incorporeal world of our creative life, while at all times staying present and concentrated in the Goethean sense of the word.

A Meditation

When Andrei Kirillov in his 'counter-provocation' quoted in the Preface said that 'Chekhov's theatre likes dreamers, idealists who desire and have time for *meditation*', he may have been using this last idea at least in part metaphorically, since the creative process – as long as we do not rush or allow the intellect to grab the steering wheel – is inherently meditative. However, at the studio we have explored an actual meditation model that can be a beautiful way of training the dynamic of connecting/experiencing and then 'stepping back' and receiving. This meditation is based on two modes of attention that are illustrated in the sketch in Figure 40.

First we focus our attention on some subject, an image, a phrase, part of a poem, there is no limit so long as it is not too complex and can be held by one's attention. It can have more than one part, say two or three images or lines of text, to be considered in turn in order to form a whole. Then, once this focus has run its course and we are ready to move on, a turning point will present itself that can feel like flipping around or turning 'inside out'. We continue to be with

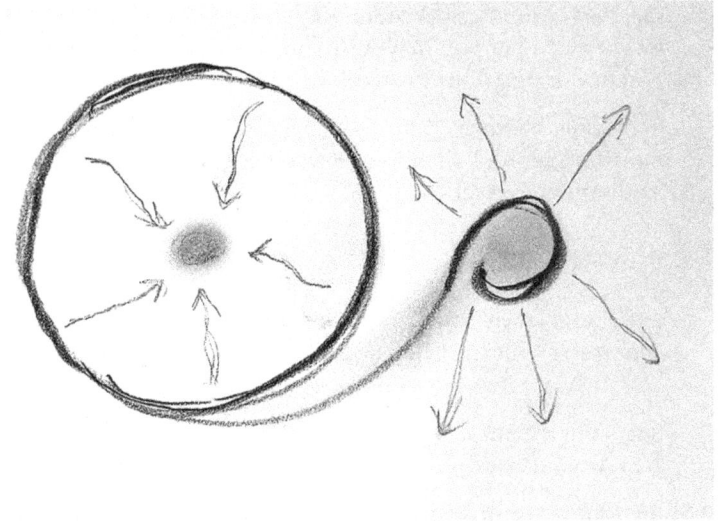

FIGURE 40 *Focused and open attention in meditation. Illustration by editor/author. Michael Chekhov Brasil archive.*

that same object, except now it is released from our focal attention and we enter an open attention of receiving whatever comes to meet us.[80] Here we have no expectations and in no way pull or grasp or seek anything, we just wait, fully present, welcoming the moment and all that it will gift us. Perhaps that will be nothing more than stillness, but it will be some form of genuine response to the chosen object of attention.

This will only (and only need) become fully clear in the practice itself.

Preparation:

- choose an object of meditation, something suitable that interests you. I like to work with phrases, perhaps something I've read recently, or a line from a favourite poem. As I write this I've been endlessly fascinated by D. W. Winnicott's observation: 'It is a joy to be hidden, but a disaster not to be found.'[81] This would be a great little pair of ideas for this mediation, but it could be anything, an image, a pattern or shape, a colour or texture, a painting or photograph or other work of art, any small thing(s) that can be held in our mind's eye with ease. Not only does the 'Paris Manuscript' contain a host of potential material for this activity, but you may well find useful here Chekhov's own practical suggestions for working with abstract ideas [30].
- find some room in time and space to be quiet and without interruption, and sit however you feel most comfortable for meditation, eyes closed.

The steps are as follows:

- settle and turn your attention to noticing your point of departure, your inner tempo as you set out, your thoughts and how they are flowing, your physical body and sensations.
- turn your attention to your lower body, your feet, legs and the area around your pelvis, noticing the physical experience.
- then move on to your midsection, your back and belly, chest, shoulders, arms and hands, the movement caused by the breath and other physical aspects of this part of your body.

- now come to your head and neck, again attending to the physical experience.
- soften yourself, with special attention to the tongue, jaw, neck and shoulders, and pelvis, and allow the breath to drop naturally into the body.
- turn to your inner life now and give your attention to your Will.
- then notice the world of your Feelings.
- and now your activity of Thinking.
- only now should you turn your Focused Attention to the subject of meditation that you have chosen, taking one element at a time. If it is a sentence you may take a word or idea at a time, if an image or other object, work with whatever makes sense, but delay as much as you can finally embracing the Whole.
- once this sense of the Whole is accomplished, you will perceive the natural approach of a turning point, perhaps like an impulse, and when this arrives, you simply allow yourself to 'turn inside out' to Open Attention and become a listener, receiver, greeting all that comes to meet you.
- at some point, it will be time to turn back to the world, and then you may open your eyes and end the meditation.

How long you will stay with each step will be a discovery you make each time.

From *The Metamorphosis of Artists*

Although Thaís Loureiro never had the opportunity to read the 'Paris Manuscript' herself, I know perfectly how excited she would have been by the endless revelations that have made up this journey of discovery, the destination of which has been the creation of this book. As a great artist, she knew its themes well and shared its creative vision, and I have seen Thaís constantly throughout, moving about and reading sections aloud, have heard and felt the frequent outbursts of delight at the recognition in Michael Chekhov's early text of so many of the experiences and possibilities she and I shared as artists and teachers. So while in a mundane sense it may be true to say that it is I alone who over some two years recognized and crafted the form of this book, it should also be plainly stated that not a line would nor could ever have been written or translated without its dedicatee; indeed, since her passing this undertaking has been one of the many ways I've found of staying as close as ever, as I find my way under the star of another of Samuel Beckett's better known quotes: 'I can't go on, I'll go on'.[82]

In many of her own writings, Thaís joined Chekhov and so many others in the Herculean task of attempting to express in everyday language the numinous ways of human creation, and in 2017 wrote a longish Goethe/Chekhov-inspired poem for our dear friends Fern Sloan, Ted Pugh and Ragnar Freidank at the Michael Chekhov School, in Hudson, New York.

It is fitting that the last Reflection be hers with these two sections from *The Metamorphosis of Artists*.[83]

THE ALLOWANCE

the Universe wants to penetrate
the artist's body
what if
you make some room for it
to occupy your inner corners
what if
you let the space take care
of you of your extra efforts
what if
you choose
to be
a channel between
prophecy and phenomenon
to be
a crusader for early detection of
unknown inner vibrations
to be
a reader a translator a messenger
travelling from the intangible to
the manifest world making
one become another

till one cannot tell who was born first
till we can no longer distinguish the
breath from the breather

what if
it is
already
done
once
you say
come in the door is open

THE GIFT OF NOT-KNOWINGNESS
to J. W. Goethe

oh, did you hear that?
a new organ just opened up
within me
I'm no longer separate
from what I see
the water is what navigates
the moving body

muscles bones skin are no longer a
boundary
but a place in which I rest myself
my Self is no longer a vague sense
of something vague
it is a reliable witness of the human
experiences I engage with

with
a child-like curiosity
I want to taste it
to play with
don't explain just
let me get dirty
with random colours just
let me
dream
dig
dare
free
full
fearless

for it is from the
wildest
faculties of mind
from the occult knowledge of
being and
by becoming utterly familiar with
surrounding images that

we truly contact the
hidden
universal
driving forces
behind (inside?)
the appearances
yes
sooner or later archetypal images
will hunt the artist
who is patient and curious enough
to appreciate things that aren't things
yet
forces that blossom quietly from
potential to action to
the never-ceasing striving for
transformation
which is the key to the eternity
of an inspired action
action yes
since players are
actors not feelers not thinkers

seekers

APPENDIX

Georgette Boner

Georgette Boner was a Swiss theatre director, illustrator and artist born in Milan in 1903. She grew up in Italy and Switzerland and in 1922 visited England, attending lectures by Gordon Craig and George Bernard Shaw, then the following year enrolled in the German course at the University of Zurich. In 1924 Boner spent a semester in Vienna, working under Max Rheinhardt, and while there made the acquaintance of Arthur Schnitzler, whose female characters would become the subject of her 1928 PhD dissertation.

That same year, Boner moved to Paris to join her sister Alice, who had been living and working there as an artist, began working in theatre and in 1930 created a German language acting group. In May 1931, Boner met Michael Chekhov and they started working together on a few projects, among them the ill-fated production of Le château s'éveille. In the spring of 1932, Chekhov accepted an invitation to work in Kaunas (Lithuania) and Riga (Latvia), and Boner joined him and his wife Xenia for the summer. It was during this visit that Chekhov and Boner began working on what has become known as the 'Paris Manuscript'.

Following Chekhov's heart attack in early 1934, Boner again spent the summer in Riga, then travelled with the Chekhovs and Alice to Italy. In early 1935 Boner, the Chekhovs and a group of Russian actors toured the east coast of the USA. When the Chekhov Theatre Studio opened in Dartington Hall, England in 1936, she joined Chekhov, Beatrice Straight and Deirdre Hurst there to give lectures. In 1938 Boner travelled to India, where her sister Alice was now living.

Following the outbreak of the Second World War, Boner returned to Switzerland for the duration of the conflict, and as well as directing some plays, worked as a book illustrator. Following a brief spell back in Paris after the war, in 1947 she settled in Switzerland and throughout the 1950s and for the next several decades continued working in theatre, and as an artist and illustrator, with increasingly frequent periods in India from the late 1960s onwards.

In the 1970s Boner corresponded with Deirdre Hurst du Prey about her collection of Chekhov papers and produced a German translation of *To the Actor* (*Werkgeheimnisse der Schauspielkunst*),[84] then in 1988 published her own book about the art of theatre, *Schauspielkunst*,[85] and in 1994 a tribute to Chekhov with much material from her personal archive, *Hommage an Michael Tschechow*.[86]

Georgette Boner passed away in Zurich on 26 November 1998, at the age of ninety-five.

Source: Peter Jakob, 'Boner Georgette Nachlass. Bericht zum Archivprojekt Oktober 2008 – Januar 2009'. Estate Georgette Boner archives, Zurich University of the Arts (ZHdK), Zurich, 2009, 12–3.

Michael Chekhov Brasil

In early 2010 a weekly initiative was launched in Rio de Janeiro with small groups of actors exploring Michael Chekhov's artistic legacy. This soon led to the foundation by Thaís Loureiro and Hugo Moss of Michael Chekhov Brasil, and the launch in 2012 of an ambitious year-round teaching programme that established for the first time in Brazil a permanent source of practical exploration and knowledge of Chekhov's artistic/philosophical universe. The studio's principal activities included a two-month training workshop, a series of shorter workshops on a wide variety of themes, and complementary initiatives such as the Archive, the production of translations and audiovisual material, maintaining partnerships in Brazil and overseas, and gradually a family of artists formed that endures to this day. Teaching initiatives were also created at the University of Campinas (Unicamp, initially under their Visiting Professor programme), as well as in partnership with SESC and other cultural institutions, thanks to which workshops were developed all over Brazil. In 2014 Grupo Assik was created to develop performance and this work was launched with a production of *'night, Mother*, by Marsha Norman.

In September 2019, the studio and friends in Brazil and around the world were devastated by the sudden death of Thaís Loureiro, after a short illness. The following year, MICHA Michael Chekhov Association dedicated its annual series of international summer workshops to her memory, and the Michael Chekhov School, in partnership with Michael Chekhov Brasil, published an eBook of the poem that Thaís had written for them in 2017, *The Metamorphosis of Artists*.[87] In 2022, audio and video recordings were produced of Fern Sloan reading this work.[88]

At the time of writing, Michael Chekhov Brasil has been devoting resources to new research and translations of Chekhov's work, as well as returning to some workshops. The studio continues to support and be supported by a group of dedicated artists, and Thaís's constant inspiration and guidance remains undiminished.

The Four Manuscripts

In addition to his autobiographical and other writings, Michael Chekhov produced four manuscripts for books about the actor's craft and the creative process of artists. Two of these were published in his lifetime, one posthumously in 1991, and now with the present publication we have an English language critical revision of his incomplete first endeavour. Here is a brief summary of the progression of all four works in chronological order (of creation) and their respective publication history.

1930s

1. The 'Paris Manuscript'
The subject of this book, handwritten in German between 1932 and 1934 with the collaboration of Georgette Boner, never completed and left behind in Paris in early 1935 when they went on tour to the USA. For more on the history of the 'Paris Manuscript', see the Introduction in this book.

1940s

2 . The '1942 Manuscript'
According to Deirdre Hurst du Prey, she and Chekhov began working on a book about his method almost immediately after they met in 1935, and certainly well before the opening of the Chekhov Theatre Studio in October 1936.[89] That work continued throughout the Dartington years (1936–1938), and during that period one of the members of the studio, Hurd Hatfield, also began collaborating on the text. After the move to Ridgefield, Connecticut (1939), a young teacher from New York, Paul Marshall Allen,[90] was also brought in to work on the text. All in all, three drafts of this book were completed, and when Chekhov moved to Hollywood in 1942 he took the latest version with him and tried to find a publisher. However, no one took it up and, according to du Prey, one reason for this was that it was generally considered 'too spiritual'.[91]

Nearly half a century later, in 1991, a version of this manuscript was edited by Mel Gordon, slightly abridged, and published in collaboration with Mala Powers under the title *On the Technique of Acting*.

3. О Технике Актера
Having failed to find a publisher for the '1942 Manuscript', and apparently somewhat dissatisfied with the English text (du Prey: 'perhaps [having] been misled in his choice of English by me and others'),[92] Chekhov resolved to rewrite the whole book in his native tongue. In 1946, he published this Russian work in New York at his own expense, but initially nothing very much came of this, presumably at least in part because he was still *persona non grata* in the Soviet Union.

Today it can be found in bookshops in some of the former Soviet countries such as Russia and Poland, but the only translation to date that I'm aware of is the 1998 German edition published under the title *Die Kunst des Schauspielers* [The Art of the Actor],[93] together with some of Maria Knebel's memoirs of working with Chekhov in Moscow. However, it is a matter of some regret that to date this work has never been made more widely available, for it is a wonderful book and, of the three completed manuscripts, may be the nearest we have to a 'director's cut', in the sense that it may have been the work Chekhov was most confident about. Certainly it appears to have had comparatively little external collaboration and editorial interference, if indeed any at all (something incidentally also true of the unfinished 'Paris Manuscript').

1950s
4. *To the Actor*
This must surely still today be the most influential book by Chekhov, published in New York in 1953 by Harper & Brothers, with a preface by Hollywood actor Yul Brynner and illustrations by Nicolai Remisoff. For several decades it was not just the only work available anywhere, but until the 1980s and 1990s, pretty much the only way the vast majority of actors could find out about his approach to acting.

Having said that, it may surprise some readers to know that of the three completed manuscripts, *To the Actor* may arguably have been least accomplished from the author's point of view. Deirdre Hurst du Prey certainly had misgivings, recalling in correspondence with Boner in the 1970s:

> He worked with two translators to try to translate the Russian book back to English, but they could not capture the style and I warned him much would be lost. Finally, he worked with Charles Leonard and 'To the Actor' is the result – a condensation of all that went before, but nothing like as rich as the other versions and much of Misha's wonderful imaginative way of saying things was sacrificed ... It is a popular book with college and university students and used in drama courses, so in spite of the fact that it does not reflect Misha at his most creative or inspired, it has succeeded in bringing him to the attention of the theatre public in the English speaking world, and it has been translated into both French and Spanish.[94]

Writing again to Boner a few years later, du Prey commented further:

> Much valuable descriptive material was sacrificed for the Charles Leonard version. I also realize that Joan Kahn was the editor who accepted 'To the Actor' for Harper & Row in 1953, and she undoubtedly had a hand in the cutting of the text and eliminating much of the sensitive material which was Misha's own and the loss of it limited the effectiveness of the book for many of us.[95]

In 1979, Georgette Boner herself produced a German version of *To the Actor* under the title *Werkgeheimnisse der Schauspielkunst* [Working Secrets of the Actor's Art].[96] As has already been discussed in the essay *Seelische Geste*, it is at times quite a free translation and even has some text amendments, perhaps prompted by du Prey's critical comments and certainly drawing on her own extensive experience of having worked so intimately with Chekhov on the 'Paris Manuscript', all those years before.

To the Actor was translated into Spanish (1955), French (1967), German (1979), Italian (1984) and Portuguese (1986), and more recently there has been a fresh flurry of editions in translation: Mandarin, Hebrew, Turkish and Serbian, to name four that I can recall offhand from the past few years.

Further Study

This book may have awoken an interest in aspects of Michael Chekhov's legacy beyond the scope of many acting workshops traditionally on offer, and point to further study generally. For anyone wishing to supplement their work by seeking further in this direction, here are a few suggestions.

The Chekhov Theatre Studio Sessions/'Actor is the Theatre' archive

Since December 2020, the vast archive of Deirdre Hurst du Prey's typed class and lecture transcriptions (which in the early 2010s took my partner Thaís Loureiro and I three annual visits to New York to digitize manually) has been freely available online. It is a treasure trove for getting a sense of Chekhov's own personal way of presenting and exploring the actor's 'lofty task', and while there is plenty of material commenting on scene work which is likely of limited interest nowadays, one never has to rummage for long in this archive before coming across gems that can be deeply inspiring. I would strongly recommend using it as a source and resource for practice and reflection:

https://collections.uwindsor.ca/chekhov/

The following sessions that Thaís and I have brought to class in various ways over the years may be a good place to start:

5 October 1936, 16 March 1937, 28 September 1937, 14 March 1938, 28 March 1938, 10 May 1938, 21 July 1938, 3 October 1938, 16 January 1939, 23 January 1939, 18 February 1939, 2 May 1939, 7 July 1939, 28 September 1939, 2 October 1939, 5 October 1939, 25 January 1940, 27 June 1940, 26 August 1940.

This online version is the copy of the archive that du Prey presented to the Leddy Library at the University of Windsor, in her native Canada, in 2002, when she was already well into her nineties (she lived to the grand age of one hundred).

Eurythmy

The discovery, training and practice of the canon of basic Eurythmy exercises can be incredibly enriching (not only for actors, of course) for awakening and connecting to rhythms and directions of our *seelisch-geistig* inner life that Chekhov recognizes as so important. But depending on where you live, it may not be easy to find a teacher of the Curative Eurythmy exercises that we have found most relevant to our work. Also, attending regular sessions over time may require a financial commitment that some might find a challenge.

However, although online work is certainly not ideal, there are two excellent teachers with videos on YouTube that are well worth exploring:

1) Theodor Hundhammer's channel *Eurythmy4you* offers well-produced videos in several languages, and the English language channel can be found here: https://www.youtube.com/@eurythmy/videos

    In the essay Thinking Feeling Willing we made reference to an exercise called threefold walking, which may be a good starting point: https://youtu.be/E1YvqgwB2SA (generally the older videos of the basic exercises are likely to be of greater interest to newcomers).

2) American eurythmist Cynthia Hoven's videos have less-polished production values but her conducting of many of the exercises is truly wonderful (see for instance the Peace Exercise and the 2020 webinars):

    https://www.youtube.com/@eurythmyonline/videos

Alexander Technique

Although I believe most people come to the Alexander Technique because of some ailment, very often back ache or what they consider to be bad posture, it should really be seen more as a preventive practice for recovering the good use of our bodies generally. In the arts, the Alexander Technique has gained widespread popularity among professional musicians, and for actors it is particularly useful for at least two aspects of our work: freeing our own physical and emotional habits to make way for rich characters to themselves develop, very much in the spirit of what Chekhov writes in the Movement section of the 'Paris Manuscript' under the subtitle 'The body defines imaginary forms' [33]; and also by offering a clear path for the challenge of expressing a character's tensions without actually becoming emotionally and physically tense ourselves.

In our 2015 production of Marsha Norman's play *'night, Mother* we had our Alexander teacher working with the actors immediately prior to each performance, and this was especially important for Thaís, whose Jessie had a great deal of tangible physical tension, especially around the shoulders and head, and reproducing a naturalistic expression of this aspect of the character for over an hour and a half every night would have been both exhausting and unhealthy. Thanks to the Alexander work it was possible for Thaís to create her character's perceived state of physical and emotional turmoil, without ever abandoning the first of the Four Brothers, the Feeling of Ease.

Like Eurythmy, studying Alexander can be a challenge, both in terms of finding a teacher and the financial commitment, but if you do have the opportunity to do so, I highly recommend it. It is also encouraging that in recent years a growing number of books about Alexander for actors have been published, among them two books by Bill Connington: *Physical Expression on Stage and Screen* (London: Bloomsbury, 2014) and *Introduction to the Alexander Technique* (London: Bloomsbury, 2020).

Speech Training

All the work actors develop in forming a *seelisch-geistig* and physical whole for their creative work, and especially when working with Chekhov's world of inner gesture, must be integrated through our breath and speech. Chekhov was fundamentally inspired by Rudolf Steiner's Creative Speech, or speech formation, and indeed this work has direct links to Eurythmy. It is a vast subject that I would encourage all actors to seek out and explore, although yet again, depending on where you live, finding a path may be a challenge. Starting places might include the article by Jane Margaret Gilmer

'Michael Chekhov's Imagination of the Creative Word and the question of its integration into his future theatre',[97] and Theodor Hundhammer's interview with Dawn Langman 'Why we should pay attention to the zodiac in acting and eurythmy': https://www.youtube.com/live/hM8FPaDj-qY

In our own work at the studio we have been greatly inspired by two teachers working specifically with integrating Creative Speech, Eurythmy and Michael Chekhov: John McManus (from Australia, now living and working in the United States) and Sarah Kane (UK).

Goethe Project

This is an online tutorial we produced in 2020 during the first months of the Covid-19 pandemic that covers the same ground as the essay Goethe's Method for Observing Natural Phenomena:
 https://www.youtube.com/playlist?list=PLbVc9R0gO_YBYvRqanuaqoloS9GQoZx_1

Academic Possibilities

This book is not capital-A academic in essence, but as I've dipped into some of the themes concerning Chekhov's language, it has occurred to me that the period 1934–6, as he transitioned from Russian and German to English, might point to further research, and indeed of the formation and language of the English canon of his texts generally (also of the Russian language adopted in the 1946 publication and other works). Furthermore, the present text underwent a series of scholarly peer reviews, with one reviewer putting forward the suggestion of 'making a comparison of Chekhov's ur-text to contemporary Chekhov training syllabi'. I gladly pass on these possible avenues of academic study to whomever it may concern.

NOTES

Epigraph

1 E. M. Cioran, *The Trouble with Being Born*, trans. Richard Howard (New York: Arcade Publishing, 1998), 45.

Preface

2 In 1977 Deirdre Hurst du Prey completed a typescript of these notes, collecting them in an archive in Dartington Hall, UK (now held at the Devon Heritage Centre, Exeter), with copies donated to several libraries in the United States (and later to Windsor, Canada – see also Appendix: Further Study in this book). Between 2011 and 2013 Thaís Loureiro and I digitized the copy in New York for the Michael Chekhov Brasil archive: Deirdre Hurst du Prey, 'The Actor is the Theatre: A collection of Michael Chekhov's unpublished notes and manuscripts on the art of acting and the theatre: typescript', Billy Rose Theatre Division, New York Public Library, 1977.
3 Andrei Kirillov, 'Michael Chekhov and the Search for the "Ideal" Theatre', in *New Theatre Quarterly*, 22(3) (2006), 227.
4 Ibid., 228.
5 Chekhov himself anticipated precisely this danger as far back as the 'Paris Manuscript' [52].
6 Aldous Huxley, *The Perennial Philosophy* (New York: Harper Perennial Modern Classics, 2009), 171.
7 Idries Shah, *Knowing How to Know* (London: IFS Publishing, 1998), 51.

Introduction

8 Research for this book unearthed two of the manuscript pages assumed to be lost, but which were filed among other material in the

Estate Georgette Boner archives, and they measure 22 × 17 cm (these are the images reproduced on pages [68] and [84]).
9 One such note reads: 'What follows is a long piece about '<u>word</u>' and the <u>meaning of sound</u>. But for now I'll leave this work until I am able to return to you what you've just sent. I'll start on the theme of 'Individuality' and then send everything back in one go. Today (2nd January) I am back in Kaunas.' Michael Chekhov, 'Pariser Manuskript, 1932–4', Boner Georgette Nachlass, Archiv ZHdK, Zurich University of the Arts, 36.
10 Michael Chekhov, *The Path of the Actor*, ed. Andrei Kirillov and Bella Merlin (Abingdon: Routledge, 2005), 187.
11 Michael Chekhov to acting group in Riga, 20 March 1934. *Literaturnoe nasledie*, vol. 1 (Moskow: Iskussstvo, 1995), 414.
12 Chekhov, *The Path of the Actor*, 188.
13 Ibid., 189.
14 In 1925, Dorothy and Leonard Elmhirst created a pioneering initiative of farming and educational projects at Dartington Hall, which by the 1930s included numerous cultural and artistic endeavours bringing together a wide variety of names from all around the world, among them Uday Shankar (also his little brother Ravi), Mark Tobey, Bernard Leach, Walter Gropius, Kurt Jooss and Sigurd Leeder, to name just a few who were at Dartington around the same time as Michael Chekhov.
15 Margareta Morgenstern (1879–1968), widow of the poet Christian Morgenstern (1871–1914). Her house in Breitbrunn am Ammersee became a retreat of sorts for Chekhov in the first years of his exile from the Soviet Union. Anthroposophist and author Michael Bauer (1871–1929) also lived there until his death and the Estate Georgette Boner archives (ZHdK) contain a printed booklet with a selection of letters revealing what an important spiritual mentor Bauer had become for Chekhov.
16 Writing to an aunt in late January 1935, Boner recounts: 'Healthwise the performances went reasonably well. *The Government Inspector* was performed twice. In the first Misha had to take nitroglycerin to fight the pain, but not in the second.' Georgette Boner to unnamed correspondent ('My dear Auntie!'), 24 January 1935, Boner Georgette Nachlass, Archiv ZHdK, Zurich University of the Arts, Zurich. Our translation.
17 In a letter to Boner in 1972, an excited Deirdre Hurst (now du Prey) wrote: 'I cannot tell you how thrilled I was—and my husband shared in my enthusiasm—when I learned that you have a draft or a book which you and Misha were writing on the technique of acting. Surely that must have been his very first attempt to describe his "method"!!'

Deirdre Hurst du Prey to Georgette Boner, 9 April 1972, Boner Georgette Nachlass, Archiv ZHdK, Zurich University of the Arts.

18 A particularly explicit instance of this is a lecture that Chekhov gave in New York on 22 September 1935, seven months after arriving in the United States (and used and adapted later at Dartington). This talk reads very much like a condensed version in English of many parts of the 'Paris Manuscript', and in particular the four sections of A Path [77–107]. 'The Theatre of the Future by Michael Chekhov. New School for Social Research, New York, September 22nd, 1935', in du Prey, 'The Actor is the Theatre', 1977.

19 Chekhov's heart condition was evidently a constant cause for concern, with Xenia writing the following account to Boner in October 1945: 'In September Misha started to have his old troubles from angina pectoris ... on the 29th he got worse, still worked but on 6th of October was in bed with a very strong attack that was very nearly fatal. For two weeks we had a doctor 3 times a day, a night nurse and consultation with his heart specialist. He was mostly under oxygen. Now little by little he is gaining strength and can sit up for a short time.' Xenia Chekhov to Georgette Boner, 25 October 1945, Boner Georgette Nachlass, Archiv ZHdK, Zurich University of the Arts.

20 George Shdanoff (1905–1998) was a Russian actor and director who met Chekhov in Berlin soon after the latter's departure from Moscow in 1928. In 1937, Shdanoff joined the Chekhov Theatre Studio at Dartington Hall and this was the start of their long collaboration. He is the dedicatee of the 1953 book *To the Actor*, and after Chekhov's death Shdanoff remained in Los Angeles teaching and coaching many well-known film actors.

21 The Estate Georgette Boner archives (ZHdK) contain correspondence between Boner, N. B. Volkova, director of the USSR's Central State Archives for Literature and Arts, and Maria Knebel, dealing with the matter of material being sent to Moscow, but in a list of items there is no mention of the 'Paris Manuscript'.

22 There is evidence in the Estate Georgette Boner archives (ZHdK) that matters became somewhat heated between the two camps. In an August 1978 letter Shdanoff refers to du Prey as the 'right honorable-horrible' and makes several unkind accusations. Comments by du Prey on this subject, meanwhile, are far more charitable: while not hiding her deep dismay that Shdanoff suddenly decided to send his Chekhov papers to Moscow (apparently also against Xenia Chekhov's express wishes), she writes that she and Beatrice Straight did realize that 'Shdanoff was motivated by his devotion to Misha and the desire to see him reinstated among the honored great of the

Russian Theatre'. George Shdanoff to Georgette Boner, 25 October 1978; Deirdre Hurst du Prey to Georgette Boner, 25 August 1976, Boner Georgette Nachlass, Archiv ZHdK, Zurich University of the Arts.

23   The annex of exercises that is missing does appear to at least have been started, since the final sheet of the 'Paris Manuscript' photocopy is a handwritten cover page that reads: 'The Exercises (annex), with their own numbering', and then a side note: 'But only up to page 4, the remaining exercises to follow.' (see also n. 26). A further scribbled aside with get well wishes and hoping for news of Boner's recovery indicates that this was among material Chekhov forwarded to her from the Baltic.

24   These are the pages numbered 152–5, which may conceivably already have been missing when the photocopy was made. Also, scattered through the photocopied sheets in the Zurich archive are remarks in pencil stating (in German) that a dozen or so other individual pages are absent. During my work I identified the occasional jump in the page number sequence, but no other breaks in the text, so presumably whoever added these remarks was misled by pagination marks missing from pages that are in fact present and correct (sometimes photocopy pages carry two notebook pages). And in two instances these erroneous amendments refer to pages that were filed elsewhere in the Estate Georgette Boner archives (n. 8 above).

25   The drawings absent from the 'Paris Manuscript' copy in Zurich would appear to be those reproduced in Boner's book *Hommage an Michael Tschechow* (Zurich: Werner Classen Verlag, 1994), 135–43.

26   On closer study, it turns out the text makes reference to just seventeen exercises altogether, and all but three of these come in the first thirty-five pages (one-tenth of the entire text), perhaps an indication that the inclusion of exercises was an initial idea that wasn't developed further. See also n. 23.

27   It has also struck me that this text was largely produced before Nazi Fascism had begun to cause widespread havoc across Europe, whereas by the time Chekhov was leading classes in Dartington and beyond, the evil forces that were being unleashed by German expansionism and, before long, the horrors of the Second World War, had also become a constant theme.

28   Compare for instance the section A Path – Fourth Stage [105–7] with the fourth stage of the creative process as described in chapter 9 of *On the Technique of Acting* (New York: HarperCollins Publishers, 1991), 155–8. In the 'Paris Manuscript' Chekhov is clearly writing from deep personal experience, whereas the later version is predominantly didactic in nature.

29 Kirillov, 'Michael Chekhov and the Search for the "Ideal" Theatre', 227.
30 The Estonian actor Lembit Peterson, for instance, has written engagingly about his journey of discovery of Chekhov's legacy as a young actor in 1970s Tallinn, a time when Soviet oppression meant the name Michael Chekhov couldn't even be uttered by his teachers (among them Maria Knebel, who studied under Chekhov and was close to him in the 1920s). The legacy Peterson describes being inspired by in his account 'L'ébauche d'un théâtre du futur' [The Draft of a Theatre of the Future] is predominantly and refreshingly 'spiritual', something that has evidently continued to guide not only his own work as an artist in this 'future', but the theatre that he founded and continues to direct, Theatrum. Lembit Peterson, 'L'ébauche d'un théâtre du futur', in *Mikhaïl Tchekhov/Michael Chekhov: de Moscou à Hollywood, du théâtre au cinéma*, org. Marie-Christine Autant-Mathieu (Montpellier: L'Entretemps, 2009), 448–53.
31 Samuel Beckett, *Worstward Ho*, in *Nohow On* (New York: Grove Press, 1996), 77.
32 Before carrying out any of the editing and revision work for the present publication, I did take the precaution of preparing a literal translation of the entirety of the surviving text, even including any crossed-out sections that are still legible, with detailed annotations and a list of Chekhov's German spelling mistakes that I identified during my work. This complete version has been presented to ZHdK so that in future all English-speaking researchers of the Estate Georgette Boner archives in Zurich will be able to make a page-by-page study of Chekhov's full handwritten text.
33 One substantial cut from the Rhythm chapter were pages that take as an example the Ghost scene in *Hamlet*, something Chekhov returned to in the so-called '1942 Manuscript' (published posthumously as *On the Technique of Acting*; see Appendix: The Four Manuscripts in this book), except there it was applied to Psychological Gesture.
34 See [66]. The phrase is from Goethe's 1824 essay 'Ernst Stiedenroth, Psychologie zur Erklärung der Seelenerscheinungen' (*Naturwissenschafliche Schriften*, Hamburger Ausgabe, Band 13. Munich: C.H. Beck, 1981), 38. The 'Paris Manuscript' contains two other quotes by Goethe, both from the book *Gespräche mit Goethe* (*Conversations with Goethe*) by Johann Peter Eckermann, but these are given in full, a strong indication that Chekhov had this volume with him in the Baltic.

35 In his classic work about the (mis)use of the English language, Eric Partridge writes of the word psychology: 'Be sure to use this vague term so precisely that its volatility is crystallized, for it can be distressingly ambiguous.' Eric Partridge, *Usage and Abusage* (London: Penguin Books, 1995), 259.
36 *Oxford Concise Dictionary* (1995), s.v. 'psycho-'.
37 The class given in Ridgefield on 5 October 1939 is a particularly good example. After discussing Goethe's ideas of the 'exact imagination', Chekhov embarks on an extraordinary exploration of the so-called Four Brothers, and comes to the sense of Form thus: 'We have a head as firm and round in form as the universe, if you imagine the sky and the stars and the horizon like a dome or cupola above you, you will see that your head is the center in this big cupola which is round, and every part of your head is directed to the stars, and they are sending rays into your head ... Then experience your neck as a column on which this beautiful 'universe' is resting. The head and neck belong to the universe, the lower part of the body belongs more to the earth.' Chekhov goes on to explore with the group the middle and lower body in the same philosophical-practical manner. du Prey, 'The Actor is the Theatre'. 5 October 1939 (for a link to the digital archive where the full transcription may be found, see Appendix: Further Study in this book).
38 In his 1955 lectures Chekhov says: 'Intangible means of expression are always present on the stage at every moment while rehearsing or acting. We must not forget about them. We must even think of them as the most important ones.' Mala Powers (ed.), *Michael Chekhov: On Theatre and the Art of Acting* (New York: Applause Theatre and Cinema Books, 2004), CD 4, track 3.
39 Robert Frost, 'A Servant to Servants', in *Complete Poems of Robert Frost* (New York: Holt, Rinehart and Winston, 1964), 83. And for any (grand)parents of young children I offer the alternative reference of Michael Rosen's wonderful book *We're Going on a Bear Hunt* (London: Walker Books, 1989), whose refrain expresses precisely the same sentiment as Frost: 'We can't go over it, we can't go under it, oh no! We've got to go through it!'
40 For example, Rudolf Steiner's lecture 'Die geistige Führung des Menschen und der Menschheit' is translated as 'The Spiritual Guidance of Mankind' (GA 015), and 'Die geistig-seelischen Grundkräfte der Erziehungskunst' as 'The Spiritual Ground of Education' (GA 305).
41 See n. 34 for citation.

A Memo to the Reader

42 Apropos the abrupt opening, studious readers may find it curious to note that, despite the two decades and two languages separating the two texts, and in what can only be a quirk of fate, the very first line of what survives of this long-forgotten early manuscript and that of the 1953 publication *To the Actor* are essentially identical: 'Actors have a twofold relationship with their body: enemy – friend.' ('Paris Manuscript'); 'Our bodies can be either our best friends or worst enemies' (*To the Actor*).

Reflections From the Studio

43 The phrase: 'An actor has to burn inside with an outer ease' must surely be Chekhov's most popular utterance found on social media and elsewhere online. No citation is ever given but I suspect it derives from something the American director Robert Lewis once recorded Chekhov as having said: 'The highest point of our art is reached when we are burning inside and command complete outer ease at the same time.' (Lewis attended the 22 September 1935 lecture given by Chekhov in New York and later visited Dartington Hall.) Robert Lewis Papers, Special Collections, Kent State University Library.

44 The initial contribution of the sitter to this chain of concentration should in no way be underestimated. Following one of the sittings for a portrait of the poet Louis Aragon, in April 1942, Henri Matisse wrote him a note: 'You posed like an angel, however you constantly eluded me. Behind the screen formed by the interest you were taking in my own activity, I couldn't get a sense of you. May I ask that in our next session you withdraw privately into yourself, so that I may observe an Aragon at home. All that this requires is that you take up some favourite subject of meditation. Then I may hope to be able to penetrate an Aragon essentially alone.' Henri Matisse, *Écris et propos sur l'art*, ed. Dominique Fourcade (Paris: Collection Sabour, Hermann, 1972), 179. Our translation.

45 Andrei Bely, quoted in Floyd McKnight, '"I Speak of the Imagination" The Acting Method of Michael Chekhov', in *Anthroposophy Journal*, 28 (Autumn 1978), 48.

46 Michael Chekhov, *Lessons for Teachers of his Acting Technique* (Ottawa: Dovehouse Editions, 2000; New York: MICHA, 2018), Lesson X.

47 du Prey, 'The Actor is the Theatre'. 5 October 1936.
48 See Appendix: The Four Manuscripts in this book.
49 Daily practice became known as '5 + 5 + 20', after a format that Thaís and I created to help overcome any lack of discipline. Participants of our two-month workshops were required to set aside thirty minutes of every day in order to practise (1) five minutes of silence and noticing the present moment (constructive rest); (2) five minutes to do a concentration exercise with objects; and (3) twenty minutes making the exercises and practices from the last class their own, and/or progressing with their character development etc (in other words their current acting/rehearsal practice). The times given were of course not strict, only an indication of a minimum, and there was a rule for those busy days when they realized they were in danger of skipping practice: it was permissible to eliminate (3), but the actors were still required to find ten minutes for (1) and (2), thereby at least maintaining a connection to their duty to their artistic self. Written down like this, '5 + 5 + 20' may not sound much, but in practice has proven to be an extremely powerful tool.
50 Chekhov, *Lessons for Teachers of his Acting Technique*, Lesson XIII.
51 These artworks are preserved in the archive of the Lithuanian Theatre, Music and Cinema Museum in Vilnius, Lithuania. Justina Kasponyte has provided a comprehensive account of Chekhov's work in Lithuania that includes reproductions of these fine drawings. Justina Kasponyte, 'Stanislavski's directors: Michael Chekhov and the revolution in Lithuanian theatre of the 1930s' (M.Phil diss., University of Glasgow, 2012), 23–5.
52 See n. 38.
53 du Prey, 'The Actor is the Theatre'. 25 January 1940.
54 Matisse, *Écris et propos sur l'art*, 322. Our translation.
55 Johann Wolfgang von Goethe, 'Bedeutende Fördernis durch einziges geistereiches Wort', in *Naturwissenschafliche Schriften*, Hamburger Ausgabe, Band 13 (Munich: C.H. Beck, 1981), 38. Our translation.
56 There are currently at least two online tutorials teaching precisely this interpretation of Psychological Gesture, as well as numerous variations introducing this work in ways that would I suspect surprise Chekhov (among them several showing that some of the concerns he himself expressed and that Kirillov has echoed – see [52] and p. xvii of this book, respectively – were by no means unfounded).
57 The other instances are remarks on how naturalism appeals to an audience's 'own' and 'everyday psychology' [62]; becoming acquainted with 'the psychology of different sociocultural groups'

[71] (although the word is quickly replaced by '*Seele*' a couple of lines later); and he writes that it would be 'psychologically impossible' to 'represent someone else's Idea on stage' [85].
58 See also n. 37.
59 *Theatre Arts Monthly*, 21(1) (January 1937), inside cover.
Of further historical note here is the advertisement of another colleague from Moscow teaching in New York at the time, Maria Ouspenskaya, who in the 1920s had founded with Richard Boleskavsky the American Laboratory Theatre and taught the likes of Lee Strasberg, Stella Adler and Harold Clurman. The two other teachers mentioned, Vera Soloviova and Andruis Jilinsky, were a married couple and also Moscow Art Theatre and Second Studio veterans who had been members of Chekhov's troupe for the US tour and then stayed on in New York.
60 du Prey, 'The Actor is the Theatre'. March 1935.
61 Ibid.
62 'The Theatre of the Future by Michael Chekhov. New School for Social Research, New York, September 22nd, 1935', in du Prey, 'The Actor is the Theatre'; and see for instance the quotes from 'Lessons for Teachers' on pp. 116, 120.
63 When Routledge published its revised and expanded edition of *To the Actor* (2002), an index was compiled, and while words like 'spirit', 'spiritual' and 'soul' are conspicuous by their absence from this list, the entries under 'psychology' take up no fewer than fourteen index lines that cite some eighty pages of the book. Incidentally, after becoming familiar with the language of the 'Paris Manuscript', it is an illuminating exercise to go through the English book and in each case consider Chekhov's likely choice of word had he still had *seelisch* (also *geistig*) at his disposal. Just as revealing is reading through the 'Paris Manuscript' and noticing the considerable shift in emphasis were most (if not all) instances of the word *seelisch* given as 'psychological'.
64 For more on *To the Actor*, see the Appendix: The Four Manuscripts in this book.
65 Michael Tschechow, *Werkgeheimnisse der Schauspielkunst*, trans. Georgette Boner (Zurich: Werner Classen Verlag, 1979), 61. Our translation.
66 Michael Chekhov, *On the Technique of Acting* (New York: HarperCollins Publishers, 1991).
67 This is, however, perfectly possible in a workshop environment. Our two-month Training groups always worked on a character from a play and Thaís and I would invariably distribute parts only after

participants had read and formed images of the play's whole world and its characters in their imaginations.

68 *The South Bank Show*, 'Edward Albee' [TV programme], ITV, 5 March 1995.

69 *LIVE from the NYPL*, 'Elizabeth Gilbert in conversation with Paul Holdengräber' [Internet broadcast], NYPL, 5 May 2011 (https://www.nypl.org/audiovideo/elizabeth-gilbert-conversation-paul-holdengraber-0).

70 *Great Lives*, 'Marcus du Sautoy on Jorge Luis Borges' [Radio programme], BBC Radio 4, 22 April 2014.

71 Alan Lightman, 'The Sense of the Mysterious', in *Daedalus – Journal of the American Academy of Arts and Sciences*, 132(4) (Fall 2003) (2003), 10.

72 François de Sales, *Traité de l'amour de dieu* (1616), (International Commission of Salesian Studies, online edition), 163. Our translation.

73 Chekhov himself certainly recognized a universal mastery in actors from disparate backgrounds or with different approaches to their art. The following remarks about American actor Ruth Draper are from his correspondence with Dorothy Elmhirst: 'What made me extremely happy and inspired me tremendously was Ruth Draper's performance. She is a really talented and even brilliant person. She has everything that we try to get through our Method – I would not be able to find one point in our Method which she has not demonstrated in her acting. Even the group feeling, being alone on the stage, was somehow there.' Michael Chekhov to Dorothy Elmhirst, 19 January 1939, Beatrice Straight Papers, Billy Rose Theatre Division, New York Public Library.

74 As is so often the case with Chekhov's outlook on life and art, we may recognize echoes of Goethe, who in an essay on morphology observed: 'The less complete a living being, the more its parts resemble each other, and resemble the whole. The greater completeness that is achieved by a being, the less its parts resemble each other.' 'Die Absicht Eingeleitet', Goethe, 1981. Band 13, 56. Our translation.

75 In the 'Paris Manuscript' Chekhov's discussions of naturalism and the 'Theatre of the Future' seem more nuanced than he has often been credited with, or even than we find in some of his own comments later in the United States, perhaps due in part to the many encounters there with actors who had been drawn into the world of the so-called American Method, then in its heyday.

76 Ursula Le Guin, 'The Operating Instructions', in *Words are my Matter* (Easthampton: Small Beer Press, 2016), 5.

77 See n. 37.
78 In Lesson XVI of *Lessons for Teachers of his Acting Technique* Chekhov introduces this, and the Appendix: Further Study in this book gives a link to a video teaching threefold walking.
79 Powers (ed.), *Michael Chekhov: On Theatre and the Art of Acting*, CD 3, track 8.
80 There is of course a direct correlation here with the third step in Goethe's method for observing nature, and thus with our various concentration exercises.
81 Donald Winnicott, *The Maturational Processes and the Facilitating Environment* (New York: International Universities Press, 1965), 186.
82 Samuel Beckett, *The Unnamable*, in *The Beckett Trilogy* (London: Picador, 1979), 382.
83 Thaís Loureiro, *The Metamorphosis of Artists* (Hudson: Michael Chekhov School, 2020), 19–29. (eBook: https://archive.org/details/the-metamorphosis-of-artists/mode/2up.)

Appendix

84 Tschechow, *Werkgeheimnesse der Schauspielkunst*.
85 Georgette Boner, *Schauspielkunst* (Zurich: Werner Classen Verlag Zürich, 1988).
86 Georgette Boner, *Hommage an Michael Tschechow* (Zurich: Werner Classen Verlag Zürich, 1994).
87 Loureiro, *The Metamorphosis of Artists*.
88 Ibid., read by Fern Sloan, published online at: https://studio.michaelchekhovschool.org/courses/metamorphosis-of-artists.
89 Deirdre Hurst du Prey to Georgette Boner, 9 April 1972, Boner Georgette Nachlass, Archiv ZHdK, Zurich University of the Arts.
90 Paul Marshall Allen (1913–1998) would go on to become the first great authority in the USA on Anthroposophy, having been introduced to Rudolf Steiner's work by Michael Chekhov during their encounters at Ridgefield.
91 Deirdre Hurst du Prey to Georgette Boner, 9 April 1972, Boner Georgette Nachlass, Archiv ZHdK, Zurich University of the Arts.
92 Ibid.

93 Michail A. Čechov, *Die Kunst des Schauspielers* (Stuttgart: Urachaus, 1998).
94 Deirdre Hurst du Prey to Georgette Boner, 9 April 1972, Boner Georgette Nachlass, Archiv ZHdK, Zurich University of the Arts.
95 Deirdre Hurst du Prey to Georgette Boner, 24 October 1978, Boner Georgette Nachlass, Archiv ZHdK, Zurich University of the Arts.
96 Tschechow, *Werkgeheimnesse der Schauspielkunst*.
97 *Theatre, Dance and Performance Training*, 4(2) (2013), 204.

BIBLIOGRAPHY

Beckett, Samuel. *The Beckett Trilogy*. London: Picador, 1979.
Beckett, Samuel. *Nohow On*. New York: Grove Press, 1996.
Bely, Andrei. *The Winds of the Caucasus*, quoted in '"I Speak of the Imagination" The Acting Method of Michael Chekhov' by Floyd McKnight, in *Anthroposophy Journal*, 28 (Autumn 1978).
Boner, Georgette. *Bilder. Texte. Theater*. Zurich: Museum Reitburg Zürich, 1996.
Boner, Georgette. *Hommage an Michael Tschechow*. Zurich: Werner Classen Verlag, 1994.
Boner, Georgette. *Schauspielkunst*. Zurich: Werner Classen Verlag, 1988.
Brook, Peter. *The Empty Space*. London: Pelican Books, 1972.
Cechov, Michail. *All'attore*. Florence: La casa Usher, 1984.
Čechov, Michail A. *Die Kunst des Schauspielers*. Stuttgart: Urachaus, 1998.
Čechov, Michail A. *Leben und Begegnungen*. Stuttgart: Urachaus, 1992.
Chejov, Michael. *Al Actor*. Mexico City: Editorial Diana, 1955.
Chekhov, Michael. *Être acteur*. Paris: Olivier Perrin, 1967.
Chekhov, Michael. *Lessons for Teachers of his Acting Technique*. Ottawa: Dovehouse Editions, 2000; New York: MICHA, 2018.
Chekhov, Michael. *Lessons for the Professional Actor*, ed. Deirdre Hurst du Prey. New York: Performing Arts Journal Publications, 1985.
Chekhov, Michael. *Literaturnoe nasledie*. Moskow: Iskussstvo, 1995.
Chekhov, Michael. *On the Technique of Acting*. New York: HarperCollins Publishers, 1991.
Chekhov, Michael. *Para o ator*. São Paulo: Martins Fontes, 1986.
Chekhov, Michael. 'Pariser Manuskript, 1932–1934, bearbeitet von Georgette Boner', photocopied manuscript, 2008. Boner Georgette Nachlass, Archiv ZHdK, Zurich University of the Arts, Zurich.
Chekhov, Michael. *The Path of the Actor*, ed. Andrei Kirillov and Bella Merlin. Abingdon: Routledge, 2005.
Chekhov, Michael. *To the Actor*. New York: Harper & Brothers, 1953; London: Routledge, 2002.
Cioran, E. M. *The Trouble with Being Born*, trans. Richard Howard. New York: Arcade Publishing, 1998.

de Sales, François. *Traité de l'amour de dieu*. First published 1616; online edition, International Commission of Salesian Studies.

The Drama Review 'Michael Chekhov', 27 (3) (1983).

du Prey, Deirdre Hurst. 'The Actor is the Theatre: A collection of Michael Chekhov's unpublished notes and manuscripts on the art of acting and the theatre: typescript, 1977'. Billy Rose Theatre Division, New York Public Library, New York.

du Prey, Deirdre Hurst. *The Training Sessions of Michael Chekhov*. Interview with Peter Hutton, Theatre Papers Third Series. Exeter: Arts Documentation Unit, 2004.

Fowler, H. W. *A Dictionary of Modern English Usage*, ed. Sir Ernest Gower. Oxford: Oxford University Press, 1983.

Frost, Robert. *Complete Poems of Robert Frost*. New York: Holt, Rinehart and Winston, 1964.

Gilmer, Jane Margaret. 'Michael Chekhov's Imagination of the Creative Word and the question of its integration into his future theatre', in *Theatre, Dance and Performance Training*, 4(2) (2013).

Goethe, Johann Wolfgang von. *Werke* (Hamburger Ausgabe). Munich: C.H. Beck, 1981.

Great Lives, 'Marcus du Sautoy on Jorge Luis Borges' [Radio programme], BBC Radio 4, 22 April 2014.

Huxley, Aldous. *The Perennial Philosophy*. New York: Harper Perennial Modern Classics, 2009.

Jakob, Peter K. 'Boner Georgette Nachlass. Bericht zum Archivprojekt Oktober 2008 – Januar 2009', archivist's report. Boner Georgette Nachlass, ZHdK, 2009.

Kasponyte, Justina. 'Stanislavsky's directors: Michael Chekhov and the revolution in Lithuanian theatre of the 1930s'. M.Phil thesis, University of Glasgow, 2012.

Kirillov, Andrei. 'Michael Chekhov and the Search for the "Ideal" Theatre', in *New Theatre Quarterly*, 22(3) (2006).

Le Guin, Ursula. 'The Operating Instructions', in *Words are my Matter*. Easthampton: Small Beer Press, 2016.

Lewis, Robert. Robert Lewis Papers. Kent State University Library, Ohio.

Lightman, Alan. 'The Sense of the Mysterious', in *Daedalus – Journal of the American Academy of Arts and Sciences*, 132(4) (Fall 2003).

LIVE from the NYPL. 'Elizabeth Gilbert in conversation with Paul Holdengräber' [Internet broadcast], NYPL, 5 May 2011. https://www.nypl.org/audiovideo/elizabeth-gilbert-conversation-paul-holdengraber-0.

Loureiro, Thaís. *The Metamorphosis of Artists*. Hudson: Michael Chekhov School, 2020. eBook. https://archive.org/details/the-metamorphosis-of-artists/mode/2up

Marowitz, Charles. *The Other Chekhov*. New York: Applause Theatre & Cinema Books, 2004.
Matisse, Henri. *Écris et propos sur l'art*, ed. Dominique Fourcade. Paris: Collection Sabour, Hermann, 1972.
Mittelsteiner, Crista. 'Georgette Boner and Michael Chekhov', in *The Routledge Companion to Michael Chekhov*, ed. Marie-Christine Autant-Mathieu and Yana Meerzon. Abingdon: Routledge, 2018.
Naranjo, Claudio. *Psicologia da Meditação*. São Paulo: Instituto Thame, 1991.
Partridge, Eric. *Usage and Abusage*. London: Penguin Books, 1995.
Peterson, Lembit. 'L'ébauche d'un théâtre du futur', in *Mikhaïl Tchekhov/ Michael Chekhov: de Moscou à Hollywood, du théâtre au cinéma*, org. Marie-Christine Autant-Mathieu. Montpellier: L'Entretemps, 2009.
Powers, Mala (ed.). *Michael Chekhov: On Theatre and the Art of Acting*. New York: Applause Theatre and Cinema Books, 2004.
Shah, Idries. *Knowing How to Know*. London: IFS Publishing, 1998.
Theatre Arts Monthly, xxi(1) (January 1937).
The South Bank Show, 'Edward Albee' [TV programme], ITV, 5 March 1995.
Tschechow, Michael. *Werkgeheimnisse der Schauspielkunst*, trans. Georgette Boner. Zurich: Werner Classen Verlag, 1979.
Winnicott, Donald. *The Maturational Processes and the Facilitating Environment*. New York: International Universities Press, 1965.

INDEX

Bold type indicates pages in the 'Paris Manuscript'.

acting technique
   general **28**, **52**, 121
   special **28–9**, **100**, 123
Albee, Edward 135–6
Alexander Technique 163–4
artistic individuality **52–5**, 75, 85, **105–7**
   awakening **55**, **66**, 85
   chooses *Gestalt* **53**, 122
   rising up to meet **52**, 123, 136
   Weltanschauung and **55–6**
artistic lies (on stage) **46–7**
atmosphere **45–7**
   artistic lies and **46**
   audience and **45–6**, 107
   play's score of **92–3**
   radiating **46**
   Weltanschauung and **92**

Bauer, Michael 167n15
Beckett, Samuel 13, 152
Beethoven, Ludwig van **56**
Bely, Andrei 115
Beuys, Joseph 12
biographies, study of **69–70**
Boner, Alice 5
Boner, Ambros 1
Boner, Georgette 156–7
   Chekhov, early partnership with 1
   in Italy 5
   in Riga 1–4
   'Paris Manuscript' collaboration 1–7, 10, 120, 156, 168n18
   To the Actor translation 133, 157, 161
   US tour 5, 156
Borges, Jorge Luís 137

character
   actions (will stream) **93–4**
   composition **94–5**
   destiny **67–71**, **81–2**, **92**
   embodying, experiencing **98**, **100**, **102**, 123
   empathy for **96**
   Gestalt and **73**, **100**
   sense of **70**, 136
   significant **81–2**
   sociocultural **71–2**
   type **74**, **82**, **92**
Chekhov, Michael. *See also* Michael Chekhov Technique; 'Paris Manuscript'; Psychological Gesture; 'Theatre of the Future'; *To the Actor*
   Boner, Georgette collaboration 1–7
   German, command of 9–10
   Hamlet performance 115

INDEX

heart problems 2, 7, 168n16, 168n19
'ideology' overlooked xvii–xviii, 11–3
  in Baltic 1–5
  in Italy 5
  Russian book 160
  US tour 5, 131
Chekhov Technique xviii
  appraisals of 11
  Chekhov's own teaching xvi, 162
  indifferent practice of xvii–xviii, 11, **52–3**, 174n56
Chekhov Theatre Studio 5, 116–7, 131, 156, 159, 162, 168n20
Chekhov, Xenia 2, 5, 156, 168n19
concentration 114, 116–9
  abstract idea **30**
  attention and **28–31**
  exercises 118–9, 125–6
  Gestalt and **30**, 117
  imagination and 30, 111, 118, 125
  Seele and **29**, 119
confidence 34–5
  seelisch powers, in 144
creative consciousness
  artistic individuality and **52**
  ignoring (dangers of) **36, 38, 53, 59**, 142–3
  inner lawfulness and 50
  rhythmic being **48–51**
creative process
  counter-intuitive 135, 139, 142–3
  director's **100–1**
  drawings of 120–4, 173n51
  dreams and 87, 136
  first 'love' 78, 87–8
  four stages of 77, 126, 129, 135
  intellect, keeping in check **79–80, 102**
  meditative 149
  rehearsing in imagination **95–6, 99, 102**

daily practice 118, 125, 173n49
Dartington Hall 5, 116, 130, 168n14
da Vinci, Leonardo **56**
Daykarhanova, Tamara 131
delicate empiricism. *See under* Goethe, Johann Wolfgang von
de Sales, St François 138
Draper, Ruth 175n73
dreams, dreaming, dreamers xvii, 126
  creative process and **87**, 136
  geistig, *Geist* and 19–20, 144
  Gestalt and 21, **37**
du Prey, Deirdre Hurst 5, 116, 142
  class/ lecture transcriptions xvi, 17, 131–2, 162, 166n2
  gathered Chekhov's papers 8, 168n22

Eckermann, Johann Peter **39, 78**, 170n34
Elmhurst, Dororthy and Leonard 167n14
Estate Georgette Boner archives 1, 170n32
eurythmy **41**, 145, 163
exact sensorial imagination. *See under* Goethe, Johann Wolfgang von
exercises
  concentration 118–9, 125–6
  Goethe's observation method 127–9
  meditation 149–51
  missing annex of 9, 13, 111, 169n23, 169n24
  seelisch nature of **28**

evil
  Gestalt for 74–5
  recognition of 106–7, 147
  two forms of 74
  See also good and evil

Faust. *See under* Goethe, Johann Wolfgang von
feelings
  calling up 87, 96–8
  form around *Gestalt* 98
  personal vs. transformed 96
forces, positive and negative 147–8
four stages of the creative process. *See under* Creative process
Frost, Robert 19

Geistig, Geist 10, 17–21
  concrete world and 66–7
  creativity and 63–6
  distinct from *seelisch, Seele* 19–21, 144, 171n37
  geistig workers, actors as 69, 109
Gestalt(en) 21, 46, 73–5, 86, 100
  actor becomes one with 105
  'disappears' 104
  evil, for 74–5
  feelings form around 98
  merge, ability to 40
  imagination and 33–4, 37–40, 73–4, 79, 122
  observation of 89, 95–6
  questioning 66, 89–90, 95
  space and 35
  synthesis and 39
  transform, ability to 39, 99
  type 39
Goethe, Johann Wolfgang von 39, 78, 127, 152, 170n34
  delicate empiricism 127
  exact sensorial imagination 16, 21, 66, 128, 171n37
  Faust 81–3, 90
  method for observing nature 117, 127–9, 165, 176n80
  morphology 175n74
  good and evil 70, 74–5, 82–3, 92
Grünewald, Matthias 112

habits 32, 47, 73, 86, 99, 164
Hamlet (Shakespeare) 54, 90, 94, 98, 170n33
  Moscow production (1924) 115
hatred in the world 72
higher creative consciousness. *See* Creative consciousness
Hurst, Deirdre. *See* du Prey, Deirdre Hurst
Huxley, Aldous xviii

idea, artistic
  author's 77, 79, 85–6
  dynamic form 83–5
  embodiment of 62, 85
  geistig nature of 77
  inner ground, artist's 39
  play's 80–5, 89, 107
  theatrical performance, vs. 77
imagination, images 37–40, 66, 121–2, 135, 141–2
  concentration and 30, 111, 118, 125
  Gestalt(en) 37–40, 73–4, 79
  'lawfulness' of 40
  independent life of 37–8, 136–7, 139
  mechanistic art and 65
  observing in world of 73–4, 79, 94, 101
  organ of awareness 37
  physical body and 33–4
  space and time, altered sense of 74
  trusting 136–7, 139, 143

individuality. *See* Artistic individuality
inner artistic 'laws' **50–1**
inner creation before outer **102–4**
inspiration **30–1**, **38**, 120, 123–4, 128–9, 139
  fourth stage creative process **105–7**
  negative parts and **106–7**
  sailing analogies for 138
  threefold nature 146–7
intellect, reason **36**, **58–9**, **64**, **67**, **94**
  creative process and **79–80**, 140
intuition, artistic **33**, **51**, **67–70**, **72**

journal, keeping 85

King, Martin Luther, Jr. 12
King Lear (Shakespeare) **53**, **82**, **90**
Kirillov, Andrei xvi–xviii, 11, 149
Knebel, Maria 168n21, 170n30

Le Guin, Ursula 141–2
'Lessons for Teachers' (Chekhov/du Prey) 116, 120, 132
Lewis, Robert 172n43
Life and Encounters (Chekhov) 2
Lightman, Alan 138
Loureiro, Thaís xvi, xix, 17, 111, 117–8, 130, 152–5, 158

Macbeth (Shakespeare) **82–3**
Maid of Orleans, The (Schiller) **82**, **98**
materialism **58–9**, 114, 139
  challenge for artists 140–3
Matisse, Henri 127, 172n44
means of expression **52**, **67**
  atmosphere 45
  concentration and 118
  inner laws of **51**
  intangible 18, 123, 171n38
  movement and **32**
  naturalistic **59–62**
  Weltanschauung and 58
mechanistic art **64–5**
meditation xvii, 149–51
Merchant of Venice, The (Shakespeare) **53–4**
Metamorphosis of Artists, The (Loureiro) 152–5, 158
Michael Chekhov Brasil xvi, 111, 116, 130, 158
Michael Chekhov School 152, 158
Michelangelo 56
Morgenstern, Margareta 5, 167n15
movement **32–6**
  aesthetic joy **32**
  confidence, ease **34–5**
  floating, radiating, moulding 33
  mechanistic art and **64–5**
music, analogy **51**, **72**, **92–3**

naturalism 60, 175n75
  art and **36**, **59**, 140
  audience's experience **62**
  mechanistic art **64–5**
  movement and **32**
  transitional art form **63–4**, **67**

objectives **93–4**
On the Technique of Acting (Chekhov) 135
'1942 Manuscript' 159–60
Othello (Shakespeare) **81–2**, **98**
Ouspenskaya, Maria 174n59

'Paris Manuscript'
  Chekhov/Boner collaboration 1–7
  difficulties formulating ideas 3–4

drawings in 120–4
editing work 15–7
first line same as *To the Actor* 172n42
German language 9–10, 17–9, 131
missing pages 8–9, 13, 122, 166n8, 169nn23–6
original document, whereabouts 8
readership 25, **108–9**, 111
relevance today xix–xx, 9–11, 14
translation choices 19–23
ur-texts in 7
Zurich archive copy 1, 8–9, 170n32
pause 57, 114–5
Peer Gynt (Ibsen) **81**, 90
performance, theatrical 77
  atmosphere and **45–6**
Peterson, Lembit 170n30
petite bergère, La (Henner) 112–4, 127
Powers, Mala xviii
Psychological Gesture 130–4, 173n56
  early development 3
psychology, psychological **64**, 171n35, 173n57
  audience's **62**
  Chekhov's usage 18, 130–2
  usage in *To the Actor* 174n63
psycho-physical 18, 20

radiating 52
  atmosphere **46**
  Weltanschauung 57
  whole part **74**, 115
Raphael **56**
Ravel, Maurice 140
reading aloud (of play) 77–9
rhythm **48–51**
  inner lawfulness **50–1**
  play's 86

Ridgefield studio 7, 125, 159
Romeo and Juliet (Shakespeare) 54, **82**, 98
Rossetti, Antonio 137

Schiller, Friedrich 78
Second Moscow Art Theatre (MAT2) 115
Seelisch, *Seele* 10, 17–21, **63–4**
  distinct from *geistig*, *Geist* 19–21, 144, 171n37
  gesture and **33**, 130–4
  Gestalt and **38–9**, 73–4, **95–6**
  speech, in **43–4**
  states **60**
Shah, Idries xix, 140
Shdanoff, George 8, 168n20, 168n22
Sloan, Fern 158
sociocultural groups, destiny **71–2**
space, changeable **35–6**
speech **41–4**
  mechanistic art and **65**
  training 164–5
spiritual, spirit 17–8, 120–1
  Chekhov's language 132
Stanislavski, Konstantin **74**, 77
Steiner, Rudolf 164
Straight, Beatrice 5, 116, 131, 168n22

'Theatre of the Future' 11, **51**, 66–8, 114, 139–40, 170n30, 175n75
thinking, feeling, willing 33, **63**, 144–8
  character's **70**
  cognitive experience of 145
  inspiration and 146–7
  meditation, in 151
  negative forces and 147
  positive forces 147–8

threefold walking (eurythmy) 145, 163
Weltanschauung and 55–7, 145
To the Actor (Chekhov) 117, 168n20, 174n63
    Boner's German translation 133, 157, 162
    first line same as 'Paris Manuscript' 172n42
    publication history 160–1
truth, beauty, goodness **51**
type (as in archetype). *See under* Character; *Gestalt(en)*

Unicamp (State University of Campinas) xvi, 158

Waits, Tom 137
Weltanschauung 21–2, 55–9, 109
    artistic individuality and 56–8
    development of **69–71**
    geistig toolkit, as **69**
    good and evil and 75
    materialistic 58–9, 62
    opinions vs. 55
    permeates artist's practice 57–8
    subconscious 57
    technical-professional matter **69**
    thinking, feeling, willing 55–7
Weltempfindung 22
    character's **90–2**
    in play 80–1
whole, feeling of **87–8**
will stream (play's) 93–4

Zurich University of the Arts (ZHdK) 1